# RESURRECTION
## FACT OR FICTION

### A Trial Lawyer Looks at All of the Evidence

- **LIFE'S TWO QUESTIONS**
- **PROTECT YOUR CHILDREN**
- **THE ISIS CRISIS**
- **FREE WILL & FREEDOM**
- **MEANING OF LIFE**
- **PREJUDICE AND INEQUALITY**
- **CHRISTIAN EXCLUSIVITY**
- **CHRISTIAN CHRONOLOGY**
- **GOSPEL FACTS**

*"Resurrection: Fact or Fiction, is an interesting and compelling blend of logic, debate, and historical information from both scriptural and secular sources. Shining through it all is a genuine concern for the spiritual state of every individual as it relates to the resurrection of Jesus Christ"*

*Westbow Press Editor*

# Wilbur McCoy Otto

**WESTBOW**
PRESS®
A DIVISION OF THOMAS NELSON
& ZONDERVAN

WestBow Press books may be ordered through booksellers or by contacting:

WestBow Press
A Division of Thomas Nelson & Zondervan
1663 Liberty Drive
Bloomington, IN 47403
www.westbowpress.com
1 (866) 928-1240

ISBN: 978-1-4908-8377-9 (sc)
ISBN: 978-1-4908-8379-3 (hc)
ISBN: 978-1-4908-8378-6 (e)

Library of Congress Control Number: 2015909318

Print information available on the last page.

WestBow Press rev. date: 7/30/2015

# Contents

# Dedications

First and foremost, this book is dedicated to the service of our Lord and Savior, Jesus Christ.

We also dedicate this book:

To the many victims of prejudice and inequality in this World, past and present, and the unsaved souls in our families and the world.

To Peggy, deceased but alive with the Lord, beloved wife of Roger and mother of Matthew, sister of Tammy, whose wrongful death case in California required much travel, capturing critical blocks of time to work on this book.

To Nancy, my wife and partner for fifty-seven years.

To our four faithful children Mark, Christiann, Jennifer and Stephen, who have delighted us by seeing each of them become better lawyers and parents than I ever was, adding to our family their wonderful life-mates, Lori, Peter, Gene and Amy, and giving us nine precious grandchildren, Joshua Mark, Luke Joseph, Lea Marie,

Gabriella Nicole, Alexia Grace, Jacob Sebastian, Kiera Jane, Bridie Kathleen, and Matthew John.

To sister Dodie, brother Richard, brother-in-law Charles, and all of our families' parents and grandparents, including, in particular, Mary, Kathy, Juanita, Marjorie, Pearl, Richard, Charles, Sebastian, and Joe.

To Will Franklin, my grandfather and great grandson (times six) of John Franklin (brother of *the* Ben Franklin), who raised thirteen children with his great, discipling wife, Naomi, who read to the family daily from the Bible (the only book the family owned) in the Great Smoky Mountains at Crossnore, North Carolina. Will was distrustful of "formal education," and he was upset when his firstborn, McCoy, became the first of many to leave home upon reaching 21 out of a desire to get a formal education. McCoy went on to become an ordained minister and a highly sought speaker and preacher. Despite Will's total lack of formal education, he built, largely with his own plans and hands, several buildings in his community. At age sixty-five, to honor McCoy's return to Crossnore to pastor the church, Will built the incredibly beautiful stone and timber Presbyterian Church of Crossnore, a building now designated as a National Historic Landmark (see photo).

To Martin Luther, an alleged great-grandfather (times fifteen) of our family through Luther's maternal grandmother, M. Zeigler of Eisleben, Germany, whose descendent Barbara Zeigler married into the Otto side of our family in 1850 and came to reside in Harmony, Pennsylvania.

Finally, to Bonnie Gift, my loyal administrative assistant, for her many years of dedicated service and her many, many hours in helping prepare the manuscript for this book.

# Acknowledgments

We would like to acknowledge Reverend Dennett H. Buettner, Rector of Church of the Savior (COTS) in Ambridge, Pennsylvania, former lawyer and counselor, whose only client is now the chief counselor and advocate for all of us—Jesus Christ—and who gave special attention to our early manuscript.

We also acknowledge:

- Bishop Right Reverend Dr. John Rodgers, Retired Bishop, AMIA, and Dean/President Emeritus of Trinity School for Ministry;
- Bishop Right Reverend Dr. J. Mark Zimmerman, Bishop of the Anglican Church in North America, Southwest Diocese, Albuquerque, New Mexico, former Rector of Somerset Anglican Fellowship, and former Rector of St. Francis in the Fields Episcopal Church, Somerset, Pennsylvania;
- Reverend Dr. John Guest, Rector/Senior Pastor of Christ Church at Grove Farm, Sewickley, former Rector of St. Stephen's Church, Sewickley, Pennsylvania and Founding Evangelist of JGET; and

- Reverend Steve Palmer, Assistant Pastor under the Rectorship of Reverend Geoff Chapman of St. Stephen's Church, Sewickley, Pennsylvania, and for whom God has great plans.

One will not find more genuine, faithful ministers of the Gospel and witnesses to the Lord, dedicated to the Great Commission of our Lord Jesus Christ;

Finally, I acknowledge my wife, Nancy, God's greatest gift and life's help-mate, who is our resident watercolor artist. Her simple, impressionistic interpretations of Scripture illustrated in this book alone warrant attention. My wife and partner of fifty-seven years devoted herself to our marriage, raising our children and later managing a small Christian bookstore. She gave up her prolific artistry twenty-five years ago—much to the chagrin of family—and was urged by family and several dear friends to re-ignite her talent. Wouldn't you know God used this little book endeavor to inspire her return to honoring God through illustrating more of His story and marvelous creation!

# Foreword

- **LIFE'S TWO QUESTIONS**
- **PROTECT YOUR CHILDREN**
- **THE ISIS CRISIS**
- **FREE WILL & FREEDOM**
- **MEANING OF LIFE**
- **PREJUDICE AND INEQUALITY**
- **CHRISTIAN EXCLUSIVITY**
- **CHRISTIAN CHRONOLOGY**
- **GOSPEL FACTS**

A quick glance at the Table of Contents and Index of this small book will reflect the Author's presentation of a volume of cogent facts, evidence and references from both inside and outside of Scripture bearing on whether the Resurrection of Jesus is fact or fiction.

And, if fact, the author describes what this means for each one of us.

If resurrected, this is easily THE central event in all of History - past, present or future. Why? Quite simply, it is the difference for each and every one of us as to whether our earthly life -

- will have been but a "vanishing mist";

  or

- will be a mere passage-way – much like passing through a foreign country before returning to our native country, in this case Eternity!

And, by the way, this life eternal will be with a real and perfect body and doing things which you like and are able to do! Recall just one day of this short life that was really special. – now imagine all days far better and for eternity!

Should we choose to not <u>believe</u> that Jesus was resurrected - read on – because fact is fact, truth is truth and non-belief erases neither.

Whether seeker, agnostic, atheist, skeptic, religious, non-religious, young or old – this book will present facts and evidence you may have never considered or even heard about.

With the warning of 9/11 we all know that we face increasing dangers, not just somewhere else, but right here in River City, USA; dangers never before experienced, originating from both within and without. Sadly, it is our young people and our precious children and grandchildren that are at greatest risk.

Do you really think any of us can provide assured protection and safety to our children (or ourselves) through education, instruction, warnings, guns, police or armies or the eternal effort of trying to persuade peoples and nations to behave – whatever that means? No, not on your life nor theirs! In fact, there is but one and only way to <u>100% assured and guaranteed safety, life and to discover the meaning of life,</u> not just for now, but forever! It is the way announced to the World 1,985 years ago by a 33 year old Jewish man when he said:

"I am <u>the Way</u>, <u>the Truth</u>, and <u>the Life</u>." [Jn. 14:6]

# 1

# World Crises

## Ishmael v. Isaac

Virtually every generation has faced war, or the tragic effects of conflict and war, and has suffered many lives lost—most often, young lives. Although we have heard this many times before, it's like the little boy who cried wolf too often, and there is great risk that we will ignore or discount warnings of future wars. Nevertheless, biblical prophecy, which is 100 percent correct to date, predicts with great specificity a further series of crises in the Middle East, all leading up to a final battle that will bring about the destruction of much that we know today.

Whether that battle will be waged against terrorists, extremists, or groups going by another name, it is clear that the current battle lines were ordained long ago between the offspring of the two sons of Abraham: Ishmael and Isaac. While it is likely that the final battle phase will employ nuclear weaponry, which will cause some degree of fire as a means of destruction, all biblical predictions and references indicate that God Himself will provide most of the fire,[1] just as He provided the water for Noah's world-wide flood.[2] Who among us can possibly look at the history of the world and current world events and not see the coming of major crises?

More than 1,000 Bible prophecies have been proven 100 percent correct to date, and there is *no* chance that the following six key predictions/promises/clear inferences—all referenced in Scripture—will fail to materialize:

1. While Scripture is less than specific, most agree that Revelation offers no basis to believe that America will have any principal role in the final great battle. While we

---

[1] "By the same word the present heavens and earth are reserved for fire, being kept for the day of judgment and destruction of ungodly men" (2 Peter 3:5–7).

[2] God promised Noah that He would never again destroy mankind by flood, creating the rainbow (which is not the result of evolution) as the sign of His covenant and promise. (See Genesis 9:11–17.) However, in Revelation, John was told of the last battle in the tribulation period that would result in the death of "a third of mankind [not by water, but] by the three plagues of fire, smoke and sulfur"—this after previous destruction of one-fourth of all mankind—for a total loss of one half of the world population. (See Revelation 9:15–18 and 6:7-8.)

all witness America's decline from its former dominant position on the international stage, it is submitted that the fundamental reason for the absence of any major role for America once the seven year tribulation period is about to commence, will be attributable to the rapture of the church and the vast impact this will have on America's population, strength, power, and vitality at the critical hour. Prior to the tribulation America's primary vulnerability will be the potential destruction or incapacitation of our nation's military and industrial complexes by means of a hostile attack on our electronic/electric infrastructure, a strategy that is undoubtedly being planned at this moment.

2. As is almost always the case, the Middle East, and Israel in particular, will hold center stage in the final crises. Israel will have been deceptively promised protection and will be in a relatively vulnerable mode when it is initially attacked.[3]

3. The reestablishment of Israel's new homeland in 1948 was clearly foretold in Isaiah 43, Jeremiah 30, and Ezekiel 36–37. Some even contend that the precise year, 1948, can be calculated.[4] It is clear that God has promised that the re-emerged, extant nation of Israel will never be destroyed, though it will ultimately require God's miraculous rescue through fire, earthquake, and water to save it (Zech. 14).[5]

---

[3] The surest sign of the closeness of the final crisis will be when we observe that Israel has rebuilt its third temple in Jerusalem and has entered into or has been granted a seven-year period of promised peace or "protection."
[4] See *"The Israel Omen"*, by David Brennan, Teknon Publishing, 2009.
[5] It is difficult for many to understand, but we must all keep in mind that "our struggle is not against flesh and blood but against the rulers, against

4. The forces against Israel will come from among its close neighbors, but they will also include foes from many nations beyond the Middle East, including west, north, and east. (Ezek. 38–39)

5. One third of the world's remaining population after the rapture of the church will suffer death from fire, plagues, and various environmental forces (Rev. 9:15–18).

6. Finally, we are to take comfort in knowing that the faithful will be the ultimate victors under God's reign!

We should also take note of two of the great underlying themes of the Old Testament: namely, God's commands to all peoples and nations (1) to give thanks to God for all good things, as these come only from Him and not from themselves and (2) to honor and respect Israel (God's chosen people through whom He has revealed Himself to all mankind), which is particularly relevant here. These two commands come with a corollary promise by God to bless those who bless, and to curse those who curse Israel (Gen. 12:3).

## Warning of 9/11

We all remember 9/11! This was no mere isolated, evil event. While certainly not an act desired by God, God allowed this evil attack to serve as a warning to America to not abandon Israel, and

---

the authorities, against the spiritual forces of evil in the heavenly realms" (Eph. 6:12).

for America to turn (or re-turn) to Him—not ourselves—for our Nation's guidance and protection.[6]

George Washington at our Nation's founding in his first inaugural address on April 30, 1789 dedicated America's guidance and protection to God's sovereignty.[7] Unknown to many, this address was delivered in N.Y. City—then the Nation's Capital. However, not just N.Y. city, but this inaugural address was given in St. Paul's Chapel then, and it is now still standing at the corner of Ground Zero!

St. Paul's stone structure was miraculously protected by a large Sycamore tree situated between the Church and the North Tower. The tree, however was felled!

---

[6] Note: In the 1960's and over subsequent years, the Supreme Court has banned in America's schoolrooms:

- Prayer;
- Bible reading;
- the Ten Commandants; and
- "one Nation under God" in the flag pledge.

Also, since the 1960's observe the growing proliferation in the US of:
- materialism and pluralism;
- pornography and sexual activity;
- self-worship; idol worship; and
- abortions.

On September 13, 2001, Secretary Powell was scheduled to notify Saudia Arabia that America intended to support an independent Palestine state. On September 21, 2001, President Bush was scheduled to announce to the UN General Assembly America's support for a Palestinian State and support for UN Resolutions 242 and 338 which called for Israel to give up lands—including East Jerusalem—and return to the borders of Israel as they existed prior to the 6 Day War. See *"As America Has Done to Israel"* by John P. McTernan, Whitacre Press, 2012.

[7] See Deuteronomy 30:16-18

Note well that America's leadership did not accept the 9/11 warning, and instead responded with, "<u>WE [the U.S.]</u> will rebuild" – some even adding "we are defiant!" Would you believe that it is at Isaiah 9:10 and 9:11 that scripture references Israel's response to the Assyrians attack 2,500 years ago as well as foretelling America's response in 2001? On 9/12/01, the U.S. Senate Majority Leader speaking on Capitol Hill quoted this scripture by stating -

> "… the bricks have fallen down, but <u>WE</u> will rebuild with dressed stone; the fig [sycamore] trees have been felled but <u>WE</u> will replace them with cedars." [Is. 9:10]

And the Senator then added:

> "That is what <u>WE</u> will do. <u>WE</u> will rebuild and <u>WE</u> will recover."

At Ground Zero, America has not only constructed the new "Freedom" Tower higher than the Twin Towers, but also in Battery Park adjoining Ground Zero, America has:

- laid 20 tons of hewn <u>granite</u> from the Adirondacks, as a symbol of "America's strength"; and has
- replaced the stricken Sycamore tree with a large Evergreen tree [a member of the Cedar family] naming it the "Tree of Hope."

As such, both Israel 2,500 years ago, and America after 9/11/01 gave the Is. 9:10 response, ignoring the warning and adopting a prideful attitude, thereby incurring God's wrathful judgment as set forth in the succeeding verse at Is. 9:11:

"... but the Lord has strengthened ... [Israel's] foes against them and has spurred their enemies on."

Note well that in addition to the physical attack on 9/11, severe financial losses also occurred in America as a result. You may not know that the N.Y. Stock Exchange also stands adjacent to Ground Zero, and it was built on the site of Federal Hall where the first U.S. Congress met. Further, just outside is a statue of none other than George Washington, and unlike the impact on the stock market, the statue was unharmed by the attack.

In this connection, careful note should be taken of the Old Testament scriptural references to God's blessings, removal of financial debt and acts of judgment rendered at seven year intervals.[8] (See Lev. 25 re: Sabbath years.) Thus, almost to the day in September 2008, seven years after 9/11/01, the nation's worst stock market/financial decline occurred with a loss of 777 points! America will do well to take notice and give appropriate response to events yet to occur in this 2015 year, the next seven year cycle.[9]

---

[8] Note: Our Federal bankruptcy laws offer relief of the effects of one's indebtedness after 7 years.

[9] Also see "The Harbinger" by Jonathan Cahn, published by Frontline Charisma Media, 2011.

## Are Your Children and Grandchildren Safe?

While I was in Southern California recently, I saw a large poster that said, "Parents, in the event of a disaster or emergency, do you know where your children are so you will be able to get them and bring them to safety?"

Attachment to our children is perhaps the strongest emotional connection we have, though it should be exceeded by our attachments first to God and second to spouse. Even as it is God's wish that "none should perish," and as He assures us that none of His sheep will perish, so too it is a strong instinct in each of our hearts to keep our children safe and to do all we can to "save" them. If only we could.[10] Indeed, it is this supreme desire to see our children and grandchildren protected and "saved" that motivated me to write this book.

No one will be saved by us (though maybe *through* us). Ultimate protection and salvation are available to all through Jesus Christ. No matter how diligent and watchful we are, no matter what electronic devices we may employ, ultimately we ourselves can offer no final protection—and certainly not salvation—to our children. Certain and eternal salvation can come only from God. What a relief it is to know that this is an absolutely sure way to provide certain protection and salvation to our children, particularly in this world filled with danger and the certainty of great suffering in the years ahead.

---

[10] For me, and perhaps for you, the single most painful event in life is to see a child suffer from pain caused by an adult. Our Father God has surely created within each of us the same feelings and emotions that He Himself holds for His children.

Let us recall God's reminder that man's life, compared to life eternal, is but a mere mist that soon vanishes. Who among us would wish to trade this mist for an eternity? And yet many of us are doing just that![11]

## The Two Most Important Questions in Every Human's Life

Since AD 30,[12] virtually every human being has faced two important questions that he must answer before his life here on earth ends:[13]

- Was Jesus, in fact, resurrected?
- If Jesus was in fact resurrected—a fact independent of whether or not we believe it—what does that mean to me and my soul, not just here on earth but for eternity?

The first and most important question is not whether anyone in the history of the world has ever been resurrected but rather whether *Jesus* was resurrected after His crucifixion death. Accordingly, there is not a scintilla of evidence in world history to suggest that

---

[11] "What is your life? You are a mist that appears for a little while and then vanishes" (James 4:14).
[12] All dates cited throughout are approximate, and scholars will differ within a range of a few years.
[13] Those who died prior to AD 30 or without knowledge of Jesus will be judged by God according to the Abrahamic covenant; their response to the revelation of God through nature, God's creation, and creative order; and the conscience placed within each of us—or otherwise, as God's mercy determines (Rom. 1:18–23; 2:1–16; Ex. 33:19).

anyone other than Jesus was ever resurrected, including Buddha, Confucius, Muhammad, Joseph Smith or anyone else.[14]

These two questions—and mankind's quest to answer them—are not an elective. They are mandatory. Thus, if we choose not to take the "exam," or we ignore it or delay taking it, we receive a failing grade. There will be no "incompletes," no second chances, and no reincarnations.

## The Centrality of the Issue of the Resurrection of Jesus Christ

Jesus Christ's assurance of ultimate protection and salvation— and the promise of a resurrected body for eternity—for each of His children is wholly dependent on the central issue in all of history, which is also the central issue of Christianity: namely, the resurrection of Jesus Christ. Is Christ's resurrection fact or fiction?

Paul clearly expressed the central and pivotal issue of the entire gospel and Christianity as follows: "And if Christ has not been raised, our preaching is useless, and so is your faith. More than that, we are then bound to be false witnesses about God ... If the dead are not raised, then Christ has not been raised either. And if Christ has not been raised, your [our] faith is futile; you [we] are still in your [our] sins. If only for this life we have hope in Christ, we are to be pitied more than all men" (1 Cor. 15:14–19).

---

[14] Note that Lazarus, the Roman soldier's son, and the poor woman's son, among other cases, are reported in Scripture to have been raised by Jesus from death. These were temporary "resuscitations" only.

# 2

# Key World Facts, Circumstances, and Status

## Calendar Dating

This book is being written in the year AD 2015. (*Anno Domini*, or AD, means "in the year of our Lord.") This is 2019 years after the year of Jesus's birth in 4 BC. (All years before year one have been marked as BC, meaning "before Christ.") I submit that if Jesus Christ had not been resurrected after His crucifixion death—an event that quickly became known and accepted worldwide— the world's dating system would not have pivoted around Jesus Christ's birth!

## Christianity

### Pre-Resurrection

Jesus Christ was born in 4 BC and was crucified in AD 30. While few people dispute the claim that Jesus Christ was crucified, some question whether Jesus actually died, despite the lack of evidence that a wounded, barely-alive Jesus was walking around after crucifixion.[1]

Jesus Christ's ministry began in AD 27 and extended for three and a half years. During this time, Jesus Christ chose twelve apostles to work with Him, and there were thousands who knew that Jesus Christ was someone special—and maybe even the Messiah. Still, there were no "Christian" churches, temples, synagogues, meeting places, or places of worship established prior to Jesus's resurrection.

**Post-Resurrection**

Following Jesus Christ's resurrection—or widely reported resurrection—Peter worked primarily among the Jews, and Paul worked among the Gentiles. During the thirty-four-year period between AD 30 and AD 64, they and their followers were spreading the gospel, which was centered on the fact of Jesus Christ's resurrection. Christianity exploded, and Christian churches[2] were rapidly formed and spread throughout the Middle East and surrounding regions.

By AD 327, this included what is now Italy, Greece, Turkey, Germany, Britain, Lebanon, Iran, Israel, Syria, Egypt, Sudan, Ethiopia, and Armenia. Between AD 64 and AD 325, no other religion grew so fast or so far—and by *peaceful* means, unlike some

---

[1] Muslims contend Jesus was whisked directly from life to Heaven and deny that God could suffer for mortal man.

[2] "Churches" were often groups of Believers meeting in homes – i.e., home groups.

others. In this regard, the heart of Christianity was a message of peace and love that was never intended to be a "religion." Rather, it was meant to be a unique relationship between each individual and Jesus Christ, who was one of a kind, a God-man who was fully God.

The Council of Nicea under King Constantine canonized all twenty-seven books of the New Testament. By then, Constantine was not dictating a new religion; he was merely authenticating what was already the most accepted religion throughout the entire Mediterranean region. In AD 380 Christianity was declared to be the official state religion of the entire Roman Empire. Imagine it: this was just 350 years after the Romans had allowed Jesus to be crucified!

Pause here for a moment, and recognize that while Jesus, as the Jewish Messiah, did not conquer Caesar and the Romans militarily as the Jews had anticipated, in a very real sense and even more effective and meaningful manner, in the space of just 350 years:

- the Word defeated the Sword; and
- Jesus conquered Caesar in the world arena!

Christianity has continued to spread rapidly, not by violence but through the peaceful spreading of the Word by Christ's disciples throughout the world. Currently, Christianity is the fastest-growing religion within China, Korea, Africa and even Indonesia with converts estimated at five hundred million over the past seventy years.[3]

## Ishmael vs. Isaac

Note the stark difference between Christianity and other religious groups. Tradition holds that, except for John, all of Jesus's apostles, gospel authors, and closest disciples willingly gave their lives for Jesus, for they knew personally that He had been crucified and then resurrected[4]. Jesus, the founder of Christianity, died sacrificially and was resurrected, and He promised future resurrected, eternal bodies to all who would follow Him.

Contrast Christianity with any religion or group whose leader or founder did *not* die for his followers, was *not* resurrected, and did *not* promise resurrection to others. Rather, these other leaders have asked their followers to die for their religion or to kill those who refuse to follow or convert to their ways—with or without the promise of later reward.

---

[3] "And on this rock (Jesus Christ *not* Peter) I will build my church, and the gates of Hades will not overcome it" (Matt. 16:18).

[4] Paul was beheaded in Rome under Nero. Andrew was crucified in Greece. Peter was crucified (upside down) in Rome. Thomas was speared in India. Luke was crucified in Athens. Simon (the Zealot) was crucified in Britain. Mark was dragged through the streets of Alexandria. Bartholomew was crucified and beheaded in Armenia. James Alphaeus and James, brother of Jesus, were stoned in Jerusalem. James, son of Zebedee, the first Apostle to be martyred, was killed by the sword in Jerusalem. Phillip was crucified in Hierapolis. Jude was crucified in Mesopotamia. Matthias was stoned and beheaded in Jerusalem. Judas, the traitor, died by his own hand. Matthew was beheaded in Ethiopia.

Take note of the origins and prophesied destinies of the descendants of Isaac as opposed to the descendants of Ishmael.

On His spiritual side, Jesus was the Son of God. On His human side, being born of the Virgin Mary, Jesus was a descendant in the line of Isaac (born in 2066 BC), the son of Abraham and his wife, Sarah. God covenanted and promised that this bloodline would produce the Savior of the world.

Ishmael was born in 2080 BC, the illegitimate son of Abraham and his servant Hagar. From him descended Muhammad,[5] born in AD 570, who produced the Qur'an (purported to have been dictated by the angel Gabriel). God prophesied of Ishmael: "A wild donkey of a man, his hand will be against everyone, and everyone against him and he will live in hostility toward all his brothers" (Gen. 16:12). "I will make him fruitful and will greatly increase his numbers. He will be the father of twelve rulers and I will make him into a great Nation" (Gen. 17:20–21).

Further biblical prophecies are being validated and played out on the international scene before our very eyes!

---

[5] It is reported that Muhammad believed much of the Bible to be essentially accurate and uncorrupted, including the fact that Jesus was born of a virgin and ascended to heaven (though not crucified and resurrected).

## The Symbolism of the Cross

The symbol of every Christian church—and indeed, of Christianity itself—is the cross. One cannot go anywhere in the world without seeing the cross worn or displayed by Jewish Christians and others. I submit that if Christ had died by crucifixion on the cross without being resurrected, the cross would be among the most despicable symbols in the world and would rarely, if ever, be displayed. Certainly it would not be the symbol for Christianity—assuming that Christianity would even exist!

The pain of crucifixion was so great that a new word, *excruciating*, was coined in the years after Jesus's crucifixion.

Note also that it was only a brief time following Jesus's resurrection, which is celebrated on a Sunday, (even if it occurred at sun down on Saturday) that Jewish Christians adopted Sunday for their Sabbath worship.

Likewise, not long after the resurrection, Christians began to celebrate both baptism and communion rituals. Baptism represents rebirth, and the communion ritual memorializes Jesus's sacrificial death. Can you imagine this happening if Jesus had *not* been resurrected after His death? Does anyone celebrate the *deaths* of Moses, Muhammad, George Washington, or Abe Lincoln?

Of course, we must note very carefully that there *is* one person whose death we do celebrate. Jesus commanded us to celebrate His death. This is simply because His resurrection would have no meaning to us if we did not first accept the fact of His death and understand His personal sacrifice for each of us!

Naming customs are attributable to a resurrected, not dead, Jesus. To illustrate the point, consider the names of our children and grandchildren: Mark, Stephen, Christiann, Joshua, Luke, Matthew, Jacob, Gabriella, Leah, and so on. Such names as Peter, Paul, David, John, Thomas, Joseph, and Mary abound in the world. However, we don't tend to name our children Pontius Pilate, Judas, Caesar, Saul, Nero, Herod, and so on (though we may give our animals these names).

In summary, it is only the resurrection of Christ that gives meaning to the cross, the Christian church, Sunday worship, baptism and communion rituals, and the names of our loved ones—and, frankly, hope, life eternal, faith, love, freedom, and so on.

# 3

# The Crucifixion, Death, and Resurrection of Jesus Christ

The crucifixion and resurrection of Jesus Christ were fully and thoroughly passed on, reported, and recorded as contemporaneous events in notes, writings, records, and memories, and by word of mouth. Primarily, they took these forms.

- Prophecies, histories recorded by secular historians
- early memorized stories, teachings, creeds and hymns
- New Testament letters
- the four Gospels

## Prophecies

In addition to his birth and life, the crucifixion of Jesus Christ was first prophesied more than two thousand years before it occurred. It was prophesied in thorough and totally accurate detail. This is only possible through the inspiration of an all-knowing God.[1]

This prophecy was given more than 1,400 years before Christ: "And you [Satan] will strike his heel, ... he [Jesus] will crush your head" (Gen. 3:15).

Written by David in 1000 BC, some 1,030 years before Jesus Christ's crucifixion, Psalm 22 contains the following descriptions. (The words within brackets that follow the words of the prophecies are either Jesus Christ's own words while hanging on the cross, or they are reported facts surrounding the crucifixion.)

---

[1] Do you know anyone who can predict with precision even 3 of 3 specific events? The Bible contains thousands of prophecies by some 66 (57 in OT and 9 in NT) prophets and prophetesses. The great bulk of these have already come to pass, and the record is 100 percent accurate. Peter Stoner, a mathematics professor in *Science Speaks*, does a mathematical analysis of the chances of just *eight* prophecies made about one man proving to be correct. Stoner illustrates this likelihood as 1 in $10^{17}$ (seventeenth power). This is the same as the chance of a blind man correctly selecting a single marked silver dollar from among a collection of silver dollars stacked two feet high across the entire state of Texas!

As referenced, here are just eight of the 50 or more prophecies regarding the coming Messiah. He would be born in Bethlehem. He would be preceded by one announcing His coming. He would enter Jerusalem as a king on a donkey. He would be betrayed by a friend for thirty pieces of silver. That silver would be used to buy a potter's field. He would be put on trial and would refuse to defend Himself. He would be crucified with thieves (D. Limbaugh, *Jesus on Trial*, 199).

In all 27% (or 8,352 out of 31,124 verses) of the Bible contain predictive material, with a total of 737 prophetic topics. (See *"Encyclopedia of Bible Prophecy"*, J. Barton Payne, N.Y. Harper & Row.)

"My God, my God, why have you forsaken me?" (Ps. 22:1). ["My God, my God, why have you forsaken me?" (Matt. 27:46).]

"But I am a worm ... scorned by men and despised by the people. All who see me mock me, they hurl insults" (Ps. 22:6–7). [The people mocked Jesus on the cross (Matt. 27:39).]

"He trusts in the Lord, let the Lord rescue him" (Ps. 22:8). [People watching Jesus Christ on the cross said, "Let us see if Elijah comes to save him! He saved others, but he can't save himself!" (Matt. 27:43).]

"I am poured out like water, and all my bones are out of joint" (Ps. 22:14). [Water and blood gushed from Jesus's chest when pierced by a sword (John 19:30).]

"My tongue sticks to the roof of my mouth" (Ps. 22:15). ["I thirst" (John 19:38).]

"They have pierced my hands and my feet" (Ps. 22:16). [Nails were driven through Jesus's hands and feet (John 20:25; Luke 24:39).]

"Do not break any of the bones" (Ex. 13:46).

"I can count all my bones" (Ps. 22:17). [None of Jesus's bones were broken by the Roman soldiers, who would often break the legs to speed up death (John 19:36).]

"They divide my garments ... and cast lots for my clothing" (Ps. 22:18). [The soldiers divided Jesus's clothes and cast lots for his tunic (Matt. 27:35).]

Read these prophetic statements, written by Isaiah in 701 BC.

- "He was despised, and rejected by men ... He was despised, and we esteemed him not" (Isa. 53:3).
- "But he was pierced for our transgressions, he was crushed for our inequities, and by his wounds we are healed" (v. 5).
- "And the Lord has laid on him the inequity of us all" (v. 6).
- "He was led like a lamb to the slaughter and as a sheep before her shearers is silent, so he did not open his mouth" (v. 7).
- "For the transgressions of my people he was taken away" (v. 8).
- "He was assigned a grave with the wicked" (v. 9).
- "Yet it was the Lord's will to crush him and cause him to suffer, and ... the Lord makes his life a guilt offering he will see his offspring and prolong his days, and the will of the Lord will prosper in his hand" (v. 10).
- "After the suffering of his soul he will see the light of life ... by his knowledge, my righteous servant will justify many, and he will bear their inequities" (v. 11).
- "Because he poured out his life unto death and was numbered with the transgressors, for he bore the sin of many, and made intercession for the transgressors" (v. 12).[2]

---

[2] Isaiah 53 is one of the complete chapters found among the Dead Sea Scrolls, which date back to 100–125 BC. They were found by a shepherd in a cave in Israel in 1947.

There are also many prophecies regarding the resurrection of Jesus Christ. Isaiah wrote, "On this mountain the Lord … will swallow up death forever" (Isa. 25:6). "In that day … your dead will live; their bodies will rise" (Isa. 26:1). "The earth will give birth to her dead" (Isa. 26:19).

Jesus prophesied His own death and resurrection on many occasions, but His apostles failed to understand until after the resurrection. Jesus said, "Destroy this temple [my body] and I will raise it again in three days" (John 2:19). "As Jonah was three days and three nights in the belly of a large fish, so the Son of Man will be three days and three nights in the heart of the earth" (Matt. 12:40). "The Son of man is going to be betrayed into the hands of men; they will kill him, and on the third day he will be raised to life" (Matt. 17:22–23).

Much like the resurrection of Jesus, the total accuracy of Bible Prophesy is itself undeniable and clear and convincing evidence beyond any reasonable doubt of the one and only true God. It is much like the man who built a wall 6 feet wide and 3 feet tall. When asked why wider than tall, the man said, "First, because the wall is unlikely to ever fall, but should it ever be overturned it will be even taller than before." [3]

## History Recorded by Secular Historians

Flavius Josephus, a Jewish secular historian born in AD 37, made two primary references to Jesus in his *Jewish Antiquities*, written

---

[3] See *"Bible Prophecy"* by Mark Hitchcock, Tyndale House, 1999.

between AD 75 and 95. The first reference (at 18:3:3) says, "At this time there was a wise man called Jesus ... his conduct was good, and he was known to be virtuous ... Pilate condemned him to be crucified ... But those who had become his disciples did not abandon his discipleship. They reported that he had appeared to them three days after his crucifixion and that he was alive. Accordingly, he was perhaps the Messiah ... the tribe of the Christians ... has not disappeared to this day."

Josephus's second reference (at 20:9:1) says, "Convening the judges of the Sanhedrin, he (Albinus) brought before them the brother of Jesus, who was called the Christ, whose name was James and some others ... he delivered them to be stoned."

While most scholars believe the first reference is largely authentic, some believe that it contains some minor Christian interpolations. The second reference is accepted by all.

Most Jews believed and accepted the fact that Jesus's tomb was found empty. See also the book entitled *Toledoth Jesu*, written in AD 500. It states, "Search was made and he was not found in the grave where he had been buried."

In addition to Scripture, Justin Martyr wrote a book in AD 150 called *Dialogue with Tryphs*. Chapter 108 reported that the Jews were teaching that Jesus's body had been stolen and that the tomb was empty.

Cornelius Tactitus (ca) 100 AD writes in his <u>Annals</u>, history of Roman Emperors: "Christus, from whom the name (Christians) had its origin, suffered the extreme penalty during the reign of Tiberius at the hand of ... Pontius Pilatus ..." (Annals 15:44).

<u>Pliny the Younger</u>, Roman legate writing to Emperor Trajan noted that "Christians were refusing to reverence Caesar's image, met regularly and sang hymns 'to Christ as if to God'" (Letters 10:96:7).

<u>Suetonius Tranquillus</u>, librarian, referenced Claudius "banishing the Jews from Rome ... Christus being their leader."

See also similar references to "Christians" in <u>Eusebius's</u> *Ecclesiastical History* and <u>Origen's</u> *Contra Celsum*.

## God and Creeds

Note the following incredible testimony from the lips of Paul himself. It witnesses to the fact that he had received the gospel and Word of God, not from man but by direct revelation from Jesus.

> I want you to know, brothers, that the gospel I preached is not something that man made up. *I did not receive it from any man; nor was I taught it; rather I received it by revelation from Jesus Christ.* You have heard of my previous way of life in Judaism, how intensely I persecuted the Church of God, and tried to destroy it. I was advancing in Judaism beyond many Jews of my own age and was extremely

zealous for the traditions of my father. But when God, who set me apart from birth and called me, by his grace, was pleased to reveal his Son to me so that I might preach him among the Gentiles, I did not consult any man, nor did I go up to Jerusalem to see those who were Apostles before I was but I went immediately into Arabia and later returned to Damascus. Then after three years I went up to Jerusalem to get acquainted with Peter, and stayed with him fifteen days. I saw ... only James, the Lord's brother. I assure you before God that what I am writing you is no lie. (Gal. 2:11–20, emphasis added).

It is believed that 1 Corinthians 15:3–8 is the oldest New Testament Scripture to be clearly referenced among common creeds that existed from the time of Jesus Christ's resurrection in AD 30. It was passed along from person to person until it was set forth in Scripture in AD 50 by the apostle Paul: "For *what I received, I passed on to you* as of first importance that Christ died for our sins ... was buried ... was raised on the third day and that he appeared to Peter, then to the twelve ... After that he appeared to more than five hundred of the brothers at the same time, most of whom are still living ... then to James, then to all the Apostles, and then last of all he appeared to me also" (1 Cor. 15:3–8, emphases added).[4]

---

[4] In *Jesus Remembered* (Erdmans, Grand Rapids, 2003), James D. G. Dunn writes that the resurrection of Jesus was tradition that was incorporated within creeds, most likely "within months" of Jesus's crucifixion. Gerd Lüdemann, an atheist scholar, acknowledges that the creeds that referenced the reported post-resurrection appearances of Jesus were

A Creed believed to be sung as a very early Christian Hymn likely within the first two years after Jesus's crucifixion:

> "Who being in very nature God … at the name of Jesus every knee should bow in heaven, and on earth and under the earth, and every tongue confess that Jesus Christ is Lord, to the Glory of God the Father" (see Phil. 2:6-11).

## New Testament Letters and the Four Gospels

The New Testament letters and books are filled with descriptions, reports, and eyewitness accounts of the crucifixion, death, and resurrection of Jesus Christ. Here are some key things to note.

---

indeed contemporaneous, going back to before Paul's conversion (Gerd Lüdemann, *The Resurrection of Christ* [Amhurst, N.Y.: Prometheus, 2004]).

These writings include incredible details and are in total agreement with each other on all major facts. Any minor reporting disparities, which are to be expected from different witnesses and reporters, only add to the believability and credibility of the writings.

The four Gospels, including the three Synoptic Gospels, are not identical, but they are thoroughly cohesive and unified. This is true of all Scripture and is possible only because God is the master editor in chief. The Gospels are close enough in major detail to be deemed true and credible, especially understanding that they are reported by four very different writers. Matthew and John were the only apostles to write the Gospels. (Matthew was a tax collector and shrewd judge of character and credibility. John was the youngest apostle and a fisherman. He was present at Jesus's interrogation by Caiaphas and at the crucifixion, and he was the first man to arrive at the empty tomb.) Luke—a physician, friend of Paul, and fact-finding scientist—stated that he had carefully *investigated* that which he was writing about. Mark[5] had the bulk of his writing dictated to him by his close companion, the apostle Peter.

---

[5] Some critics claim that Mark's gospel is "corrupted," because the last twelve verses of Mark 16 were not included in the earliest versions of the book. Note well that in the previous verses, Mark noted that the three women (Mary Magdalene, Mary, and Salome) found Jesus's tomb empty and that a young man in a white robe told them not to be alarmed, and said, "He has risen, he is not here. See the place where they laid him … go tell his disciples … he is going ahead of you into Galilee; there you will see him just as he told you." The last twelve verses go on to cite some of the appearances of Jesus, the Great Commission, and Jesus's ascension. Also note that Mark made no references to himself being at any appearance of Jesus.

The fact is that the twenty-seven letters and books of the New Testament are without major conflict or disagreement between them, despite being written by eight different human reporters[6] over a period of some fifty years between AD 40 and 90. Further, these writings were completed and passed around within a relatively brief period—seven to sixty years—following Jesus Christ's death and resurrection. This occurred in an era when writing and copying documents was all done by hand, a feat that was nothing short of miraculous.

Additionally, in the culture of that time—and completely contrary to our own culture—oral accounts, not written accounts, were considered the best evidence. The apostles and their disciples only resorted to writing their accounts when it became apparent that the Christian movement would outlast their lifetimes. It was therefore necessary to do something while they were still living on earth to perpetuate their testimony for future generations.

As it was in the case of the creeds, much of the material, if not most, had been passed along orally, over and over again. Much had also been written down in notes, and the creeds and notes were all used to write the final letters and books. Thus, it is safe to say that much, if not most, of the material appearing in the final, printed letters and books originated from day one (or should we say, day three), having been preserved in the creeds, notes, minds, and stories of the writers and the people, immediately following the resurrection of Jesus Christ.

---

[6] Matthew, Mark, Luke, John, Paul, Peter, James, and Jude.

Finally, all of these activities, writings, and stories occurred in a world with fewer agendas, and unlike today, those agendas were fully disclosed.

## Lapse of Time between Events, Reports, and Recordings

Many people have the impression that the Bible, including the New Testament, records events that occurred many years— even decades or centuries—earlier. Even if the time lapse were great, this would not necessarily impact truth or accuracy. Historically, while human error is unpreventable, the custom of telling and retelling facts, news, events, and stories—especially within a culture that revered accuracy and objectivity far more than reporters do today—favors accuracy and credibility. Further, the true miracle of Scripture is that God, in His sovereignty, is able to take broken, sinful, human agendas and eras and use them to bring about His best purposes for people and for His world.

In the case of the crucifixion and resurrection of Jesus Christ, any time lapse was virtually nonexistent for the immediate creeds and hymns and was likely as short as seven to ten years in the case of Matthew's gospel and the letters to the Thessalonians and Corinthians. All of this took place within a small space of time and place and at a time when the purpose of the culture and style was to report events accurately and truthfully, with little or no spin.

Take note that stories reported about the deaths of more recent figures—such as Lincoln, Kennedy, and King—not only occurred immediately but continued for over one hundred to one hundred and fifty years, with later efforts often revealing even more facts. Certainly, no one disputes whether or how Lincoln, Kennedy, and King were killed, nor the accuracy of the basic facts. Of course, in the case of Jesus, the only reason Jesus's crucifixion and death were highlighted and reported in detail was because Jesus was resurrected, an unprecedented event that would have been first reported and written about immediately!

## Overall Chronology of Key People, Events, Reports, Writings, and Old and New Testament Letters and Books[7]

| | |
|---|---|
| 3000 BC | The great flood, Noah, and the rainbow |
| 2800 BC | Stonehenge, UK |
| 2700 BC | Discovery of writing |
| 2500–2000 BC | Reports, stories, writings, and creeds leading to Old Testament books |
| 2166 BC | Abram (Abraham) born |
| 2080 BC | Ishmael born to Abraham and Hagar |
| 2066 BC | Isaac born to Abraham and Sarah |
| 2050 BC | Abraham offers Isaac to God as sacrifice |
| 1750 BC | Babylonian/Hammurabi Code |
| 1526 BC | Moses born |
| 1446 BC | Exodus from Egypt |
| 1456 BC | Ten Commandments authored by God[8] |
| 1446–1406 BC | Moses writes Genesis |
| 1000 BC | Psalm 22 and David |
| 965 BC | Solomon |
| 780 BC | Jonah |
| 753 BC | Founding of city of Rome |
| 701 BC | Isaiah 53/Assyrians besiege Jerusalem |
| 600 BC | Jeremiah |

---

[7] All dates are approximate. Many precise dates are unknown, and scholars differ considerably within a fair range. However, for purposes of this chronology, it is the order of events that is more illuminating rather than the precision of dates.

[8] A bookstore in Manchester, VT has engraved in its stone entry, "Nothing is written in stone!" How wrong in so many respects!

| | |
|---|---|
| 587 BC | Babylonian Exile/1ˢᵗ Temple destroyed |
| 563 BC | Buddha born |
| 560 BC | Daniel |
| 551 BC | Confucius born |
| 539 BC | King Cyrus of Persia captures Babylon |
| 500 BC | Zechariah |
| 450 BC | Ezra assembles "Hebrew Scriptures," of which several thousand "copies" exist today |
| 448 BC | Athenian power |
| 350 BC | Codex Sinaiticus found in St. Catherine Monastery, Mt. Sinai, in 1859, which includes most of Old Testament |
| 332 BC | Tyre destroyed by Alexander the Great[9] |
| 250–200 BC | Septuagint Greek translation of Hebrew Old Testament by seventy to seventy-two Jewish scholars |
| 100–150 BC | Dead Sea Scrolls: Accurate scroll copy of Isaiah and other OT Books copied by Essenes found in cave in Khirbet Qumran, Israel, by shepherd |
| 100–44 BC | Julius Caesar |
| 70 BC | Cicero |
| 63 BC | Pompey captures Jerusalem |
| 27 BC | Octavius 1ˢᵗ Roman Emperor |
| 5/4 BC | Jesus Christ's birth, the pivotal point in history |

---

[9] The Bible's thousands of prophecies, all proven accurate to date, included the fact that the cities of Tyre and Babylon would be destroyed and would never be rebuilt (Jer. 51:26, 62–64). Note that Saddam Hussein once threatened to rebuild Babylon, and Saddam did not fare well. In any event,

| AD 1 | Paul and John born |
|------|-------------------|
| 26–36 | Pontius Pilate, procurator of Judea |
| 29 | In the temple, Jesus reads from Isaiah and references the writings regarding the Law of Moses, the Prophets, and the Psalms (Luke 24:44–45) |
| 30 | Jesus Christ's crucifixion and observed/reported appearances following His resurrection |
| 30–31 | Creeds referenced in 1 Corinthians 15:3–8 |
| 31 | Peter begins ministry and spreading of gospel |
| 32 | Stephen martyred |
| 33–34 | Jesus Christ appears to Paul on the road to Damascus, and Paul is converted from killing Christians to becoming one |
| 35 | Paul's Conversion |

---

neither city has been rebuilt to date, and if we ever see Tyre or Babylon rebuilt, we can argue that the Bible is all wrong.

| | |
|---|---|
| 37 | Matthew's gospel, argued by many scholars to be the earliest[10] |
| 37 | Flavius Josephus born (AD 37–100) |
| 40 | James, son of Zebedee, is the first of the apostles to be killed for his faith. |
| 40–45 | Paul's letter to Thessalonians and then Philippians written and reproduced (within ten to fifteen years of Jesus Christ's crucifixion and resurrection) |
| 52 | Thalus's History (see Africanus below in 221) |
| 55 | Paul's letters to Corinthians and Romans |
| 57 | Mark generally believed to have written the first of the four Gospels (some believe Matthew was written first) |
| 59 | Gospel of Luke |
| 60 | Book of Acts |
| 62 | Paul's letter to Timothy |
| 62 | James, brother of Jesus, dies for the faith that he gained only upon learning of Jesus's resurrection |
| 64–68 | Matthew's gospel |
| 66 | Paul is beheaded (time of Nero) |
| 67 | Peter crucified upside down |
| 70 | Romans under Titus destroy the second Jewish temple and virtually all of Jerusalem[11] and the Jews were dispersed from their homeland for the next 1,878 years |

---

[10] Simon Greenleaf, *The Testimony of the Evangelists*, 29.

[11] Despite the fact that one or more of the Gospels may have been written after AD 70, a good argument can be made that since none of the four Gospels reference the huge event of the Roman destruction of the second

| | |
|---|---|
| 82 | *Antiquities of the Jews* authored by Josephus |
| 88–90 | John's gospel |
| 90 | Council of Jamnia confirms the Old Testament canon |
| 90–93 | Each of the four individual Gospels—written previously—are in wide circulation well within sixty years, and many within twenty to twenty-five years of Jesus's resurrection |
| 100 | John dies |
| 150 | A book containing all of Paul's letters, except Titus and Timothy, are in circulation |
| 150 | Justin Martyr |
| 156 | Polycarp killed for his belief in Christ[12] |
| 160 | Irenaeus of Lyon (studied under Polycarp) canonizes the four Gospels |
| 200 | Earliest known compilation of all four Gospels published |
| 221 | Julius Africanus's History, referencing Thalus |
| 300 | Codex Vaticanus and Codex Sinaiticus Bibles in existence |
| 325 | Council of Nicea under Constantine canonizes the entire New Testament. |

---

Jewish temple in AD 70, all four gospels were almost assuredly written *before* AD 70. It is recognized that one might argue the fact that since the three Synoptic Gospels record the prophecy that the temple would be destroyed in AD 70, and assuming that these Gospels were written *after* AD 70, it would therefore be unnecessary and redundant to record the fact of the AD 70 destruction event. However, the counter-argument is that it would be even more compelling to do so, showing the prophecy's fulfillment.

[12] "Eighty and six years I have served Him, and He hath done me no wrong. How can I speak evil of my King who saved me?"

| | |
|---|---|
| 380 | Roman Emperor Theodosius issues the edict of Thessalonica, which establishes Christianity as the official state religion. Even earlier, Christianity was made the official religion by Armenia and Ethiopia |
| 390 | Jerome's Vulgate Bible |
| 401 | Augustine's *Confessions*, Patricus taken into slavery, Germanic invasion of Roman Empire |
| 432 | Bishop Patrick arrives in Ireland |
| 570 | Muhammad born |
| 632 | Muhammad dies, Qur'an appears (alleged to have been largely dictated by the angel Gabriel) |
| 1291 | Fall of Acre to Muslims |
| 1384 | Wycliffe's English Bible |
| 1450 | Guttenberg printing press (first book printed is the Bible) |
| 1516 | Erasmus NT (Greek/Latin) |
| 1517 | Luther's "Ninety-Five Theses," beginning of Reformation |
| 1522 | Luther's NT (German) |
| 1525 | Tyndale's NT (English) |
| 1539 | English "Great Bible" (Henry VIII) |
| 1560 | Geneva Bible (Colonial America's favorite) |
| 1611 | King James Bible (thanks to Tyndale who was burned at the stake in 1536) |
| 1787 | Ben Franklin held the Constitutional Convention together by suggesting prayer before each session |
| 1948 | Israel reestablished as a Nation |

The book of Thomas, along with other gnostic and apocryphal books, did not appear until AD 175 or later, and none were ever canonized, although they were contained in many of the first Bibles, including the Geneva Bible.

## Key Observed, Reported, and Recorded Facts and Events Surrounding Jesus's Crucifixion and Death

1. Relative to Jesus Christ's crucifixion, few people today question or can even raise doubt as to whether Jesus Christ was in fact crucified. This includes the great majority of all scholars, believers and nonbelievers alike.

2. Relative to whether Jesus Christ in fact died on the cross, very few people contend that Jesus did not die, and those who do can offer no credible explanation of what happened to a severely wounded Jesus or what He

looked like if He did not die. The facts are clear that Jesus spent much of one day hanging suspended upon a cross with His arms outstretched and bones coming out of joint. The effect this has on the body's ability to breathe, particularly exhalation, after a very short time, is certain and devastating. Further, the reported and recorded observation of a Roman soldier piercing Jesus Christ's side and causing blood and water to gush out of Jesus's lungs is a telling detail that only God would record—not only for the detail but to demonstrate its scientific accuracy. Jesus's death was essentially the result of asphyxiation and hypovolemic shock. This caused His lungs to fill with fluid (pericardial and pleural effusion), which explains the gush of both water and blood from Jesus's side. Jesus's statement on the cross, "I am thirsty" is symptomatic of both hypovolemia and dehydration.[13]

---

[13] See John 19:28. Also see chapter 11 in Lee Strobel's *The Case for Christ*, which sets forth the comments and opinions of Dr. Alex Metherell, a physician and engineer. I have known Dr. Metherell personally for a number of years, and his medical and scientific background, together with his long study of the Bible, qualify him as an expert. His opinions eliminate all reasonable doubt as to the fact of Jesus's death on the cross. We must not fail to note the many incredible scientific truths that are contained in the Scriptures, two of which are captured here by the "water gush" and "I am thirsty" facts. Both are thoroughly consistent with the consequences and symptoms of crucifixion.

While there are many other scientific or medical examples, we note here two further examples. First, only in recent years has medical science discovered and confirmed that the human body's highest blood coagulability occurs on the eighth day of life. Is it any wonder that in the Old Testament God called for all Jewish boys to be circumcised on the eighth of life? (See Genesis 17:12.)

Note that the Roman soldiers broke the legs of many victims to expedite their deaths, but they did not need to do so for Jesus.

3. One of Jesus's seven phrases, spoken on behalf of his human side while He was on the cross, was "My God, my God why have you forsaken me?" (Matt. 27:46). If one were writing the story and seeking to falsely promote Jesus Christ as Lord and Savior, indeed as resurrected God, one would not likely choose to report a comment that would initially appear to many to be disingenuous, inconsistent, and even blasphemous—unless, of course, it was true and fully consistent with Jesus's being fully man and fully God.

4. Finally, the fact that Jesus was incarnated and came to earth primarily to serve as man's perfect sacrificial lamb and die for man's salvation is accepted by virtually all. One of the earliest phrases quoted and written (and tattooed!) after Jesus's death was "born to die."[14]

---

Second, DNA was discovered only in recent years. DNA includes a precise and certain universal blueprint of man's genetic characteristics. It is a master blueprint that is so detailed, organized, systematic, and certain that it would be impossible to explain by evolutionary process. If one accepts the notion that DNA evolved, such willingness to place faith in a belief devoid of cognitive process is both whimsical and baseless.

[14] First, think of a time in your life when you were in pain, hurt, offended, upset, or unfairly or unjustly treated. Most often this was a consequence of your own action or conduct. Now visualize and meditate for a single minute of Jesus's experience in hanging on the cross in excruciating pain—pain totally undeserved—having never sinned or done anything wrong. He hung there, not because of his own conduct but for the misconduct and failures of all others, including you and me. After a moment or two of

## Old Testament Blood Sacrifice

From the earliest times in the Old Testament, God required bloodshed through the sacrifice of an animal offered to God as a substitutionary sacrifice for the redemption of human sins and atonement with God. "For the life of a creature is in the blood and I have given it to you to make atonement for yourselves … it is the blood that makes atonement for one's life" (Lev. 17:11).

Why did God require this shedding of blood and substitution of life for life? Certainly, it was not because God had some strange or bizarre thirst for blood or death.

Rather, all of this was designed by God as a periodic reminder of people's sins and their need for redemption and atonement ("at-one-ment") with God. It was also meant to point ahead to the coming, ultimate, final sacrifice and shedding of blood that would take place with God's Son, Jesus. The shedding of Jesus's blood gave full and clear meaning to sacrificial death and the shedding of blood for one and all, once for all time.

Take note that God meant for this ultimate sacrifice and shedding of blood to be the last and final shedding of blood that would be necessary as a substitutionary sacrifice for all, regardless of race or nation. Each of us who personally accepts this sacrifice of Jesus's life as substitutionary on our behalf and in our place is

---

considering this, is it not true that your own pain, if not gone, has at least become bearable?

41

thereby provided personal forgiveness of sin, justification, and atonement with God.

Then God went two steps further and *resurrected* Jesus, thereby providing the *first* resurrection. God promises a second resurrection: eternal life to all who accept Jesus's life sacrifice as substitution for their own lives. (See Genesis 4, 22.)

## Cain and Abel

One other key point to note about this substitutionary blood sacrifice in the Old Testament is the fact that not just any sacrifice would suffice. Rather, the sacrificial animal, typically a lamb, had to be spotless and without blemish or defect, as perfect as possible. Why was this necessary?

Again, this was a forerunner to and a foretelling of the coming of Jesus Christ, the lamb of God, and the most wholly (and holy) perfect sacrifice possible. The fact that the final sacrifice and shedding of blood for all of mankind had to be through the most true and perfect sacrifice possible meant that it could only come through God's sacrifice of Himself through His Son, Jesus, as one person of the triune God. Thus, Jesus, being God incarnated as man, had to come to earth—first to teach and model the Christian life, and then to be our perfect sacrifice and die for us!

Cain's offer of a sacrifice to God consisted of farm produce and lacked the shedding of blood. Unlike Abel's sacrifice of an animal,

Cain's offering was unacceptable to God. Cain went on to kill his brother Abel, and he was condemned to permanent death and separation from God.[15]

## Abraham and Isaac

The most clear and dramatic precursor of the coming of Jesus Christ as a sacrifice for us is the incredible story of Abraham and his intended sacrifice and shedding of blood of his only son Isaac, the promised son he had waited for until he was nearly a hundred years old. In obedience to God's command, which was a test of Abraham's faith and trust in God, Abraham was about to shed Isaac's blood when God stopped him. Suddenly and miraculously, God provided for Abraham a ram caught in the nearby brush, and thereby provided an animal blood sacrifice for Abraham. As a result, God provided to Abraham what God would later deny to Himself, namely an escape from the sacrifice of his son. God's testing of Abraham found him to be totally obedient and trusting toward God. How many of us would have been found so? Praise God for not requiring such a test of us! (See Genesis 22.)

After reading these stories in the Old Testament—which occurred and were written some two thousand years before Jesus's crucifixion, shedding of blood, and death—it would be difficult to conclude that anyone other than Jesus Christ, the Messiah, could ever be the perfect sacrifice for the sins of us all. Further, God's blood covenant

---

[15] See Genesis 4.

and promise of resurrection were extended to all who would claim this substitutionary sacrifice of Jesus Christ as their own.

With today's high emphasis on self-esteem, self-pride, self-justification, and tolerance of all conditions and lifestyles, it's less difficult for people to believe in the *fact* of the transforming process of Jesus's substitutional sacrifice, than it is for people to believe that they have a *need* for it!¹⁶

## Key Details of Reported and Recorded Evidence, Events, and Facts Regarding Jesus Christ's Resurrection

Take note that the facts and events along with the specific details surrounding Christ's resurrection lend high credibility and believability to the account. Consider the following eighteen examples.

1.  Three outside environmental events, one of which is verified outside of Scripture, occurred as Jesus was dying on the cross.

    • A curtain, or veil, separated the innermost Holy Place from the rest of the temple in Jerusalem. The Holy Place was a sanctuary entered only by the chief priest on special occasions. It symbolized the "seat of God." While Jesus was on the cross, the veil was torn in two, down the

---

¹⁶ "If we claim to be without sin we deceive ourselves and the truth is not in us" (John 1:18). If we are not in Christ, "all our righteous acts are like filthy rags" (Isa. 64:6).

center from top to bottom—the opposite direction in which such a curtain would be most likely to tear.

- The ground shook, and many graves in the vicinity were suddenly opened, raising their contents from the dead.
- The afternoon sun disappeared, and the skies were totally darkened for several hours throughout the Middle East and beyond.

Historian Julius Africanus (AD 221) referenced the works of historian Thalus (AD 52) in stating the following: "At the time of Jesus' crucifixion on the whole world there pressed a most fearful darkness; and the rocks were rent by an earthquake, and many places in Judea and other districts were thrown down … a darkness that appeared without reason. An eclipse of the sun takes place only when the moon comes under the sun; how then should an eclipse be supposed to happen when the moon is diametrically opposite the sun!" (See Africanus's and Thalus's report in *History of Eastern Mediterranean* about an inexplicable darkening throughout the Middle East at the time of Jesus Christ's crucifixion.)

2. Jesus Christ made seven statements while on the cross:

- "My God, my God, why have you forsaken me?" (Matt. 27:46).

- "Truly, I tell you, today you will be with me in Paradise" (Luke 23:41–43) (addressed to one of the two criminals being crucified beside him).[17]
- "Father, forgive them, for they do not know what they are doing" (Luke 23:34).
- "Dear Woman, here is your son; John, here is your mother" (John 19:26).
- "Father, into your hands I commit my spirit" (Luke 23:46).
- "I am thirsty" (John 19:28).
- "It is finished" (John 19:30).

After reading the above seven statements of a man while being crucified on a cross consider also C. S. Lewis's comment about Jesus being "Lord, lunatic, or liar."

3. The body of Jesus Christ was placed in a tomb. This was not just any tomb but was one owned by Joseph of Arimethea, a Sanhedrist who was opposed to Jesus and was reportedly a friend of Pilate. Jesus's enemies would thus have known well the location of the tomb and would have had control of it.

---

[17] There is no punctuation in Hebrew. However, most Bible texts place a comma *before* "today" rather than *after* "today." Some could argue that the latter might be the correct placement. However, if in fact there is a separate "paradise" holding place prior to heaven—and surely such a place is implied—then the comma is correctly placed, and Jesus was saying that the crucified robber would be with Jesus in paradise "today" (Friday). The alternative is that Jesus was saying, "I *tell you today* that you will be with me in paradise," i.e., eventually, when He returns for the rapture of the church and all others who are "asleep" in Christ, who will be resurrected first and will then join Him in paradise, or heaven.

4. Jesus's body was wrapped in burial cloths along with one hundred pounds of spices, the weight of which alone could kill a person.

5. A very large stone was used to secure the entry to the tomb and the stone was sealed.

6. Jewish leaders placed two guards at the tomb, fearing even the possibility that friends of Jesus Christ might steal the body.

7. Matthew, at Mt. 28, reports that at dawn on the first day of the week Mary Magdalene and the other Mary went to the tomb and:

   • "there was a violent earthquake".
   • "an angel of the Lord came down from heaven, and going to the tomb, rolled back the stone, and sat on it".
   • "the guards … became like dead men".
   • "the angel said to the women … he (Jesus) is not here; he has risen, just as he said …" (also see Luke 24).

Thereafter, Jesus Christ first appeared to one woman, Mary Magdalene, and then two or three women, including Mary Magdalene, Mary, and/or Salome. They ran to tell Peter and John that the tomb was empty and that they had encountered a risen Jesus Christ.

In considering the above, recall that Old Testament Scripture always references the need for two witnesses to testify to any event or fact in any legal proceedings.

Second, women were not regarded as credible witnesses, so these women were already disqualified as legal witnesses. If the apostles had been making up the resurrection story, there was no way they would have reported that women were the first witnesses to the resurrection, because no one would have been obligated to believe their account. Accordingly, the only reason to report that women were the first to come to the empty tomb is because it was absolutely true.

## The Curse

8.  It was a curse to be hung on a tree. "If a man guilty of a capital offense is put to death and his body is hung on a tree, you must ... bury him that same day, because anyone who is hung on a tree is under God's curse" (Deut. 21:22–23).

It must already have been difficult for the writers of Scripture to record that women were first to find Jesus's tomb empty and to be told by the angel that Jesus was risen. However, this difficulty pales in comparison to reporting that Israel's long-awaited Messiah—the one who was destined to conquer all of Israel's enemies (the Romans and others) and then assume David's throne—had (uh-oh) just been shamelessly hung on a tree (cross). Given this curse, Jesus's crucifixion would be the last thing any disciple would wish to report.

So why was Jesus's hanging on a tree not only reported but fully accepted by His disciples and others? It is simply because the impact of Jesus's crucifixion was totally transformed by the further fact—a fact even then widely accepted as true—that on the third day, *Jesus was resurrected*, which meant that He was the true Messiah, the Christ![18]

9. Peter and John ran to the tomb and found the heavy stone rolled away. Upon entering the tomb, they found it empty and saw Jesus's burial cloth *neatly folded*. Why would anyone include the detail of a neatly folded burial cloth, unless it was true? If someone had stolen Jesus's body, would the thief have neatly folded the cloth? Did this cloth ultimately become the Shroud of Turin?

Q: Why the detail of the "neatly folded" burial cloth? Perhaps, there are three reasons. First, because it was a

---

[18] While the church, for many reasons, has adopted Sunday as resurrection day, there can be no doubt that Jesus was in the tomb for three whole days and three whole nights, which was just as Jesus prophesied when He referenced the story of Jonah and the whale (Matt. 12:40). Many argue that a careful reading of the entirety of Scripture supports Jesus having been crucified and dying around 3:00 p.m. on Wednesday (the "Day of Preparation" before the *annual* Sabbath) and then spending the three full nights of Wednesday, Thursday, and Friday and the three full days of Thursday (the high day Sabbath and first day of the Feast of Unleavened Bread), Friday, and Saturday in the tomb before rising at sunset on Saturday evening. Mark 16:9 states, "Now having risen, early the first day of the week He appeared first to Mary Magdalene." While the Greek has no punctuation, many interpreters have incorrectly placed a comma after "week" instead of "risen," which would tend to (incorrectly) support a Sunday morning resurrection. Therefore, when the women came to the tomb on Sunday morning, the guards were long gone, the stone had been rolled away, the tomb was empty, Jesus was not there (having risen at sunset on Saturday), and the angel(s) said, "Why do you look for the living among the dead? He is not here, he has risen" (Matt. 28).

true detail. Second, because Jewish tradition was that if a diner's napkin was thrown down unfolded, the diner was through; however, if the dinner napkin was neatly folded it signaled the diner was not finished and would return and so, too with the message intended by Jesus. Third, if someone stole Jesus's body—would they take the time to neatly fold the napkin? Finally, we wonder if this cloth was/is the Shroud of Turin?

## The Two Guards

10. How does one explain the two guards falling asleep while guarding the tomb? Guards knew that falling asleep on duty meant punishment by death.

It is likely that either the guards did not fall asleep but rather were "put to sleep" by the angel(s), or that the angel(s) shielded the guards' eyes during Jesus's resurrection.

More significantly, both Scripture and historians tell us that when these guards reported to the priests the fact of the empty tomb, they were bribed by the priests to say that they had fallen asleep and that when they had awakened, Jesus's body had been taken by His friends. This is a story that is still repeated by many Jews and others today.

What is clear is that Jesus's tomb—a tomb provided and owned by Joseph of Arimathea, a tomb that had been made secure by putting a seal around the large stone, and the posting of guards— was *empty* (Matthew 27:66). This fact remains undisputed, even by Jesus's enemies, both then and today.

One can imagine the intense search effort that was conducted in an attempt to find the body of Jesus Christ. The search effort soon ended when no body was found, and there were many reports throughout the region of Jesus's resurrection and His appearances to many people over a period of some forty days. Indeed, it was clearly accepted by many, if not most, of the people at that time that Jesus Christ had in fact resurrected. Keep in mind that at that time—outside of the Jewish Pharisees or Saducees—most had no concept of resurrection, a resurrected body, or what it all meant. Perhaps this is true for many people today.

It is interesting to consider how the gospel writers might have learned that the guards had been bribed. Perhaps at least one of the guards was converted to "the Way," or Christianity.

One Bible critic who writes behind a pseudonym states he does not believe in Jesus' resurrection because "no one actually saw him rise", and that Jesus's "means of escape is a mystery". Since only Jesus was in the tomb, sealed and with a large stone, there may have been no witness to the actual resurrection itself, beyond the three witnesses of the Trinity, but I'm guessing that at least one of the two tomb guards will one day add interesting detail to the Gospel message!

As to Jesus's "means of escape" the critic chooses to simply ignore all of the vast and otherwise inexplicable evidence of Jesus's post-resurrection appearances, together with Jesus' Ascension which he notes is "not referenced by Matthew or John."

11. The New Testament gospels and letters record that Jesus Christ, in addition to appearing to two or three women and the two men on the road to Emmaus, appeared in the upper room, first to ten apostles (Judas having killed himself) and then to the eleven, with doubting Thomas now present. Thomas, not unlike many of us today, would not believe until he had placed his fingers in the hole in Jesus Christ's side or in the nail holes of His hands and feet. In all, some eleven appearances are recorded in Scripture, and some are referenced in other historical reports. In truth, there were

likely many more, given the forty days that Jesus remained on earth before His ascension.

## A Small Miracle

12. Jesus appeared to some of the apostles, who still not believing that Jesus was Messiah, had returned to their fishing occupation by the Sea of Galilee but were catching no fish. Jesus Christ told them to cast their nets on the other side of their boat, and upon doing so, they promptly caught fish. Once ashore, they counted 153 fish. None had been lost, for their net did not break (John 21:11). Why does this account include such detail, and why were there 153 fish?

The poet Oppian later reported in his "Catalogue of the Fishes," published in *Halieutica*, that at that time, there were known to be 153 varieties of fish in the world. John's gospel record of this fish-catching event was written between AD 50 and 90, and Oppian did not write his "Catalogue of the Fishes" until AD 190 during the reign of either Commodus or Severus. This is a small but dramatic miracle of Scripture that underlines the fact that all Scripture is inspired by God. Only God could have known in AD 50–90 what number of fish categories Oppian—who was not yet born—would report more than a hundred years later in AD 190!

Why would a catch of 153 fish be otherwise significant? Because it illustrates that Jesus reaches out to *all*—all kinds, all varieties, all nationalities of people—with His message of salvation. Once they are caught in the net of Jesus Christ, that net will *not break*. None of His sheep will be lost.[19]

Now, contrast this story in John with a similar story in Luke 5:6. This was a time when Jesus had not yet died and resurrected. He was about to select his apostles to be "fishers of men." Jesus instructed Simon and the other fisherman and apostles to cast their nets into the deep. This time, "such a large number of fish were caught that the nets began to break." (Do not be a fish who is initially attracted or entangled but then escapes Jesus's net!)

13. We must not fail to see that Jesus Christ also chose this post-resurrection appearance at the Sea of Galilee to restore and redeem Peter by asking him three times, "Do you love me?"

---

[19] Jesus said, "I give them eternal life, and they shall never perish; no one will snatch them out of my hand" (John 10:28).

Jesus asked once for each of the three times people had asked Peter if he knew Jesus. While Peter had sat in the courtyard of chief priest Ananias where Jesus was being interrogated on the night before His crucifixion, three people had asked him, "Don't you know this man Jesus?" And each time, Peter had denied knowing Jesus—the very one to whom he had previously said, "You are the Christ" in response to Jesus's question: "Who do you say that I am?" (Mark 8:29; Luke 9:20).

This is a story of understandable human weakness and cowardice. It is also a story of God's amazing grace, mercy, and power to regenerate, recreate, and forgive us when we fail—if we repent and turn to Him. (See also Luke 12:9.)

Note that Peter, in order to save himself, was quick to lie and deny Jesus *before* Jesus had been crucified and resurrected. However, when Jesus's resurrection was personally confirmed to Peter, Peter did a complete turnabout. He preached to all about Jesus Christ "and him crucified and resurrected."

Further, when it came time for Nero and the Romans to kill Peter for his faith, Peter not only submitted himself to death, but he refused to be hung in the same fashion as Jesus Christ. Rather, he insisted that he be hung on the cross upside down. Imagine a person doing such a thing for something or someone if he had not witnessed or known the true, resurrected Christ![20]

---

[20] One unidentified writer suggests that Peter was on his way out of Rome when he was suddenly confronted by Jesus Christ on the road. When Peter asked, "Lord, where are you going?," the Lord replied, "To Rome to be

14. Many people saw Jesus Christ. They heard him, touched him, and saw him eat. Paul pointed out in 1 Corinthians 15:8, "Jesus Christ appeared to more then five hundred persons at one time—most of whom are still living." (And if they were still living at that time, they could have, and would have, spoken to many others, being thoroughly interrogated by the curious and the skeptic!)

As unique as such a resurrection was, Jesus's resurrection became well-known and accepted by many within this small community at that time. It is important to note that during this time, no one was known to have reported or recorded any falsity or doubt of the facts. It had been observed, reported, and known by many that (1) the tomb was empty and (2) Jesus had resurrected. His post-resurrection appearances were observed by so many that the resurrection was commonly accepted as true.

Finally, in this connection, note the following obvious, but often over-looked facts lending even greater credibility to the truth of Jesus crucifixion, death, resurrection, and multiple post-resurrection appearances:

---

crucified." The astonished and embarrassed Peter immediately turned around, returned to Rome, and was arrested. It was then that he insisted on being crucified upside down (attributed to "The Acts of Peter. a very early but non-canonical book, *"Who's Who in the Bible"*, by Readers Digest Assn. Inc., 1994.

All of the apostles and close disciples, including Paul and excepting only John, gave their lives for a Jesus they had now seen and/or knew to be resurrected. See Chapter 2, [FN4.]

- all of these events occurred within a very small, and the same geographical area in and very close to Jerusalem;
- all among the same knowledgeable people; and
- additionally, most of these events occurred within a compact period of four to seven days, and all within forty days.

## Convert the Enemy/Saul becomes Paul

15. Jesus Christ appeared to Saul, an enemy of Jesus—next to Satan perhaps His chief enemy—on the road to Damascus (Acts 9). Perhaps this was the single most impressive post-resurrection appearance of Jesus Christ, and it came *after* Jesus's final forty days. Why did Christ appear to Saul?

My military training and West Point experience help me to more fully appreciate the brilliance of Jesus as a strategist and tactician in choosing to appear to Saul.

Saul was the foremost enemy of Jesus Christ. Articulate and highly intelligent, Saul was a strong leader and teacher of Pharisee-Judaism, and he was a principal persecutor of early followers of Jesus Christ. Acts 8:1 reports that Saul was present at—and was perhaps even the instigator of—the stoning death of Stephen, Jesus's first martyr. (Stephen was yet one more follower who professed Christ after Jesus's resurrection and then gave his life for his belief.) By converting Saul (renamed Paul), Jesus Christ eliminated the chief and most articulate opponent of the Christian faith. Notice that Jesus *converted* Saul. He did not kill him! Killing enemies is a tactic employed by many opponents of Christianity.

Most importantly, by accomplishing Saul's conversion, Jesus made the reborn Paul His last apostle and recruited him to His team. He commissioned Paul to be His chosen instrument in proclaiming Jesus to the Gentiles. Thus Jesus was able to capture and dedicate to the cause of Christianity the single most important, articulate, and highly regarded Jewish teacher and leader at that time.

## The Thorn

One important postscript regarding God's frequent use of the "thorn in the flesh." Paul clearly possessed great intellect and communication skills—perhaps even charismatic. Add to that the special attention paid to Paul by Jesus himself and one can sense that human pride being chief among the deadly sins could have over-taken Paul, detracting from the Gospel message, away from Jesus and Him crucified. The answer for God—as is so often the case—was a dose of reality, humility and perspective—in this case an unidentified thorn in the flesh of Paul. Not only in allowing the thorn, but in refusing to grant Paul's three requests to remove it by saying: "My grace is sufficient for you, for my power is made perfect in weakness" (2 Cor. 12:9). I submit that Paul's thorn is unidentified in scripture, so that greater and broader application can be made to the numerous pains we humans suffer—or as my mother would say— "the crosses we must bear in our lives."

As we know, Paul would go on to write the first New Testament letters (to the Corinthians and Thessalonians). In total, he wrote thirteen of the twenty New Testament letters. During that time, he was persecuted and imprisoned on numerous occasions, yet he remained steadfast throughout and "finished the race." Ultimately, he was beheaded under Nero for his faith.

The single fact that Paul—a highly educated, committed, and dedicated Jew and the poster child for strong free wills opposed to Jesus—could be turned 180 degrees by Jesus Christ's appearance is itself a compelling fact that is responsible for converting many. It is my opinion that it was because of Paul's strong will that Jesus blinded him for three days, during which time he fasted (Acts 9:9). After three days, Jesus told Ananias to "lift the scales" from Paul's eyes. This experience, followed by additional days spent with the disciples, provided an intense time for impression, repentance, refocus, and the working of the Holy Spirit toward Paul's reeducation and reorientation.

This event must persuade anyone with an open mind and even minimal experience with human nature of (1) the miraculous power of Jesus Christ and (2) the absolute fact of Jesus's resurrection, which was so clearly, directly, permanently, and indelibly witnessed by Paul, and which motivated Paul's subsequent life of sacrificial dedication and service.

16. Let's look at two illustrations involving skeptics and committed evildoers.

**The Skeptic**

If Paul was the poster child for having strong free will and being an enemy of Jesus, James, the brother of Jesus, was the poster child for skeptics. Not unlike Joseph's jealous brothers, who tried to kill Joseph, James thought Jesus was his deluded older brother who talked strangely. James did not believe anything Jesus was saying. (One is never accepted as a prophet in his own hometown—or family.) However, following Jesus's resurrection, James instantly became a believer, assumed leadership of the Christian Church in Jerusalem, and was later stoned to death for his belief![21]

Also note that James told us in his New Testament letter, "What good is it, my brothers, if a man claims to have faith, but has no deeds? ... Faith by itself, if it is not accompanied by action, is dead" (James 2:14–17).

---

[21] Josephus referenced James as "the brother of the so-called Messiah ... who was delivered to be stoned." (*Antiquities of the Jews*, 20:9:1).

Among the many more recent and notable skeptics who were converted after investigation and study—skeptics who initially sought to disprove Jesus as the Christ—are Harvard Law School Professor of Evidence Simon Greenleaf, journalist and author Lee Strobel, [22] and attorney Chuck Colson, one of President Nixon's close advisors.

## Study – Not Blind Faith

While the God-created conscience within each of us has certainly played a significant role in leading our hearts to be opened to the Holy Spirit and the way of Christ, I would submit that the human intellect once subordinated to God's wisdom and our God given free will—to be examined further later—plays the leading role by far.

The fact of the resurrection is not a feeling, emotional response nor blind faith; it is a conclusion based on search and study, utilizing our God-given intellect, reason, and our cognitive processes to seek God's wisdom in our assessment of all of the events, people and products of history together with the world around us.[23]

---

[22] See Simon Greenleaf's *The Testimony of the Evangelists*. See Lee Strobel's *The Case for Christ*, *The Case for Faith*, and other works.

[23] Of course, the single greatest product of history is the Bible (*Basic Instruction Before Leaving Earth!*). Note *Lincoln's* comment:

"I believe the Bible is the best gift God has ever given to man. All the good of the Savior of the World is communicated to us through the Book, but for it we could not know right from wrong."

And *Immanuel Kant's:*

As such the following two observations are compelling.

First, those who have decided not to believe or make a decision relative to Jesus Christ have rarely done so after thorough study and research of all of the material events, people, and products of history and the world around them, usually for one of the following reasons:

- refusal to engage in any study due to bias, prejudice, lack of diligence[24], or a fear of the limiting effect it might have on their present life-style;
- electing to study only a selected portion of all of the available information and data thereby being side-tracked to some belief, faith, cult, or practice other than Christianity; or
- failing to seek God's wisdom in their study.

Second, even more persuasive than the above is the fact that almost everyone who has thoroughly examined all of the material events, peoples and products of history along with the world around them, have concluded that Jesus lived, was crucified, was resurrected, is the Christ, and our living God, Creator, and

---

"The existence of the Bible, as a book for the people, is the greatest benefit which the human race has ever experienced."

[24] Even Ben Franklin while believing in a Creator God and largely responsible for holding together the Constitutional Convention in June 1787 by suggesting that each day's session begin by "prayers imploring the assistance of Heaven", late in his life, admitted in a letter written to Ezra Stiles in 1790 to not having taken the time to study whether Jesus' divinity was true or not. How sad.

Savior. Even more remarkable is that most of those who engage in this study start out as skeptics, agnostics, or even atheists!

## Committed Doers of Evil

Now, let's consider some notorious evildoers. The imprisoned Boston Strangler, Albert DeSalvo, was evil personified. Like thousands of others, his heart was regenerated when he became a believer as a result of the Great Commission. That is, he heard the Word and the gospel message, opened his heart to Jesus, and was given a "heart transplant"—a regenerated heart—through the leading of the Holy Spirit.

Indeed, transformed lives are perhaps the best evidence—and perhaps the most convincing—that most of us experience or see firsthand in our own lives: namely, the ongoing power of the resurrected and living Jesus Christ. This power of heart regeneration is something that *only* the Word and the power of

Jesus and the Holy Spirit can offer. This power is available to all and has proven itself in the hundreds of thousands throughout human history who have opened their hearts to Jesus. As a result, they present themselves as living exemplars in the form of changed lives, redirected wills, and models of the love and peace of Jesus Christ. These changed lives can only be explained by newly regenerated hearts.

Most of us fall into this category of evildoers. Perhaps we are not so evil as King Herod, the Boston Strangler, or Adolf Hitler, but we are evil nonetheless. If real and meaningful change is to occur, we need the power and ability of the Holy Spirit to secure for us hope, redemption (as was offered to Peter), renewal, and a new heart.

17. Jesus performed a multitude of miracles, and the Gospels and other New Testament books record many of them. He multiplied the bread and fish to feed five thousand, an occurrence that involved so many people and was so broadly reported that it could not have been denied. He (temporarily) resuscitated people who had died, including Lazarus. Let us not do as Thomas Jefferson did and create our own version of the New Testament by eliminating all of Jesus's many miracles. We need only carefully observe the world around us and our experiences in life to recognize that miracles are real. The fact of Jesus's miracles is thoroughly consistent with His virgin birth and His having resurrected.

## Shroud of Turin

18. Is the Shroud of Turin the actual linen cloth that covered the crucified body of Jesus in the tomb?

"So Joseph [of Arimathea who provided Jesus's tomb] bought some linen cloth, took down the body, wrapped it in the linen and placed it in a tomb" (Mark 15:46). "The other disciple [John] outran Peter and reached the tomb first. He bent over, and looked in at the strips of linen. Then Simon Peter … saw the strips of linen lying there, as well as the burial cloth … folded [neatly] up by itself, separate from the linen" (John 20:4–7).

Today, the Shroud of Turin is in the Turin Cathedral in Turin, Italy, where it has resided for over four hundred years. Many believe it is the very cloth that covered Jesus's body, including his head, and then folded under his back to lie beneath his body. What appears "incredible" is that this cloth has imbedded within its fibers the image of a nude male body, including injuries to the hands, feet, and side. It also has a face that bears strong resemblance to several famous paintings of Jesus, including one by Leonardo Da Vinci. Most importantly, both the front and back images are "photographic negatives"—but photography had not yet been invented. There is also evidence of what appears to be blood residue in various portions of the cloth, consistent with the precise wounds suffered by Jesus Christ's crucified body. It would be difficult to believe that this negative image could have been painted onto or into the cloth.

In 1988 carbon 14 testing was performed. The test results concluded that the age of the cloth most likely placed it somewhere in the period between AD 1000 and 1500, which is contrary to other examinations that conclude that the cloth is much older. Keep in mind that carbon 14 dating methodology is highly controversial and certainly imperfect. Additionally, DNA testing was performed on some of the blood residue, but the DNA test results have never been released. Finally, note that a book entitled *Turin Shroud* by Picknett and Prince suggests that the Shroud of Turin may well have been a hoax created by Leonardo da Vinci (1452–1519), a highly controversial character. However, until the eighteenth century when the shroud was sealed and placed under glass, the shroud was never displayed and kept carefully secure and guarded. Investigation reflects no record of the artist ever having seen the shroud.

If the shroud is real, the unexplained photographic-flash "negative" effect—an effect that would perhaps occur at the moment Jesus's body was resurrected—would offer strong (maybe even undeniable) "photographic" evidence of a resurrected Jesus. If the shroud is a clever hoax by Leonardo—and there appears to be credible evidence in support of that —it would represent yet one more warning against placing our faith in anyone or anything other than the revealed Word of God in Scripture.

## Why did Jesus—Son of God—and God— have to die?

First, I would submit because so many feel need to ask the question!

Second, to illustrate just how much sin hurts both the sinner and the victim, sometimes even taking life.

Third, the hurt, death or debt must be adequately punished and paid for – and death may well be the only equitable price.

Fourth, punishment must be significant enough to be meaningful, effective and cause attention (ask any parent!).

Fifth, if I pay your debt, the larger your debt and the larger my payment, the more my love for you, and the greater your gratitude, relief and sense of forgiveness.

Sixth, Jesus/God did not kill another but rather gave his own life as God to show His incredible love for us, the seriousness of our sin, His willingness to pay the highest price for our sin, and to focus our attention on the righteousness and holiness of God.

Seventh, to put real meaning into His forgiveness of us, and our forgiveness of others, forgiveness must be costly.

Eighth, to illustrate the majesty of not overcoming evil with evil, fear with fear, strength with strength, rather using humility and weakness, mercy, grace, and love to produce victory.

Ninth, to transform death into resurrection and life, and illustrating this with indelible impact.

Tenth, finally to quote John Stott: "when we sin, we substitute ourself for God; when we are forgiven, God substitutes Himself for us."

# 4

# The Ascension of Jesus Christ, the Great Commission, Free Will, Freedom, and the Return of Jesus Christ

Why, after His resurrection and His appearances over a period of forty days, would Jesus Christ leave earth and ascend from the Mount of Olives to heaven?

First, though Jesus left earth, He left in His place the Holy Spirit and Comforter, the third person of the Trinity. Jesus said this was "better," in that the Holy Spirit could be everywhere, with and within each and all of us, at one time—unlike Jesus, who was at one place or with one person at a time (John 14:16–17).

Second, Jesus left to "prepare a place" for all who eventually come to Him. He will return to gather them in rapture at a future time, a time that grows closer and closer. In the meantime, Jesus

Christ leaves the Holy Spirit and people to utilize human will[1] to decide to "come to Him" by opening their heart's door, that decision itself being a gift of God. Once having done so, converts are invited to join Jesus's church army as His soldiers and disciples to carry out His Great Commission.

Third, it would be easier for Jesus Christ to simply make puppets of each and all of us and "force" us to come to Him. As He did with Paul, Jesus could appear to each of us individually! Despite the impact, importance, and purpose of Paul's experience, for Jesus to force His will on us would be totally meaningless and of no value to us, God, or His purpose. Rather, God created within each human being an independent will. God seeks and desires that each of us—through the exercise of a will that is strongly inclined toward a "human nature" that is adverse to God—with urging of the Holy Spirit to open the door of our heart to Jesus.

God allows trials and tribulations into our lives so He can use them to awaken us and bring us to Him. As children disciplined by a loving Father, we should welcome life's painful trials.[2] It is a fact that we often do not choose to open the door to our heart until we find a need to do so. That need is often produced through life's setbacks, failures, trials, pain, suffering, and other

---

[1]  This will is relatively free and is often very strong. Ever since the fall of man in the Garden of Eden, the heart is naturally human and is inclined to be oriented to self rather than God.

[2]  "And we know that in all things God works for the good of those who love Him, who have been called according to His purpose" (Rom. 8:28). "Consider it pure joy ... whenever you face trials of many kinds, because ... testing of your faith develops perseverance ... be mature" (James 1:2–4).

events and experiences that point us toward Him. Whether out of desperation, as a last resort, through prompting by the Holy Spirit, or by hearing the gospel at a time when our "soil" has been made fertile, our hearts can be opened and God's purpose accomplished![3]

In fact, the heart is regenerated through the work of the Holy Spirit, and our new spirit "motor" fills us with a new desire—or even compulsion—to serve God. However, if our new heart acts like a motor, it is the mind that functions like a steering wheel. The mind must be refocused on, or transformed to, the things of God. The computer acronym *GIGO* means "garbage in, garbage out." So it is with our minds, which must feed on God's Word.[4]

---

[3] As a result of the fall of man, our hearts are slaves that have become bonded to sin. They are pre-programmed toward our sinful, human nature and away from God. At the same time—but for a time only—Satan, the Prince of the Air, is being allowed by God to reign relatively freely in the world. Together with his demons (one third of the stars of heaven (angels) who fell out of the sky along with Satan), he encourages evil, self-pride, idol worship, and self-interest in the human heart. (See Revelation 12:4–9.)

The only way to reprogram our hearts is to regenerate or renew them (or "reboot" them, for the techies) by opening our hearts to Jesus and allowing the Holy Spirit to take control over our sinful nature. In doing so, we become bonded to God and are now slaves to Him. (I have often thought it interesting that "live" spelled backward is "evil." Perhaps it is a warning to all of us not to live backwards.)

[4] "Do not conform to the pattern of the world, but be transformed by the renewing of your mind. Then you will be able to test and approve God's will" (Rom. 12:2).

Through circumstances, events, the work of the Spirit, and the exercise of our wills, our lives are changed. Through the "domino effect" of our Christ-inspired actions and deeds, human relationships and conditions in the world are changed. This is the result of our emulation of Jesus's character and the Holy Spirit's indwelling of us. Jesus taught His disciples—and us—to do these things:

- Have a grateful heart and a humble spirit.
- Sacrifice and give of our God-given talents, time, and treasure to others.
- Love God first, and then all others, more than self;
- Be peacemakers.
- Turn the other cheek; payback no wrong for wrong.
- Be servants and provide servant-leadership.
- Forgive others.
- Trust Him, not ourselves.
- Rid ourselves of self-pride and idol worship.
- Encourage one another and build each other up.
- Give thanks in all circumstances.
- Pray continuously.

The Christian's faith is activated and actuated through selfless deeds and service to others. Critical institutions and all manner of charitable organizations and world outreach missions—such as the Salvation Army, World Vision, the Red Cross, and so forth—have been established by Christians. The forerunners of most of today's large hospital systems were founded by Christian churches. All of these have had incredible impact in providing love and care for those in need of care in the world. None of this would have occurred if not for the discipling process of changed hearts and minds in the service of Christ and the fulfillment of His Great Commission.[5]

Add to this God's patience, love, and desire that "none should perish" but that all should come to Him, and you begin to understand—and be eternally grateful for—Jesus Christ's delay in His return and the day of judgment. This gives us and all of our loved ones more time to learn to love, to become fertile "soil," and to open our hearts to God's Word, thereby illustrating to the world the truth and the only way to salvation and peace.

Jesus's objective is to first receive each of us who turns away from evil and comes to Him as His child. Then He charges each of His disciples with the Great Commission: to spread the good news of peace, love, and salvation to others. Isn't this the most powerful, impactful, and meaningful way to spread the gospel? First He creates as many disciples as possible. Then He energizes these many disciples to witness and spread the good news to others. There is nothing like "word of mouth" and firsthand witnessing of life's experiences to enhance credibility and believability. It is also yet another strong and effective "God stratagem" to overcome and conquer the Enemy "from within," which is, perhaps, particularly effective in this "wired" age.

---

[5] "We are ... created in Christ Jesus to do good works" (Eph. 2:10).

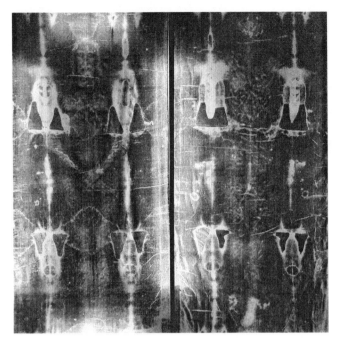

The Shroud of Turin (Wikipedia)

## Trusting in God

We cannot "have our cake and eat it too." Likewise, we cannot serve two masters. Thus, we cannot love both Jesus Christ and the world. It is not enough to simply know with our minds or intellect that Jesus is in fact the Messiah/Christ, our Savior and Creator. We must also love and obey His Word, and He (not ourselves) must be the Lord and master of our lives. As children of God, we must live in the world, but we do so as citizens of heaven traveling through the world. As we travel, we are laying up eternal, not earthly, treasures (our souls, character, knowledge of God's Word, prayers, and all of our experiences reflecting God's Word and love to others) for our heavenly home.

While God's blessings—as with sunshine and rain—fall on all, it is critical to understand that only God's children—those who have accepted and serve Jesus as Lord—possess an array of gifts. Here are some of the gifts God gives His children:

- Forgiveness of sins
- Righteousness and justification
- Reconciliation and atonement with God
- Eternal salvation and freedom from death
- Protection from the coming great tribulation in the world
- Direct communication with God through prayer
- The armor of God and protection against the unseen, but very real, evil spiritual realm
- Inner peace and joy that "passeth all understanding"
- Protection of guardian angels
- The eternal presence of Jesus Christ and the power of the indwelling Holy Spirit and Comforter in and through all of life's trials and tribulations
- The promise that "in all things God works for the good of those who love Him, who are called according to His purpose" (Rom. 8:28)
- Knowledge of true meaning and purpose of life

## Meaning of Life

Who does not search for the true meaning of life? Here it is, right before our eyes and ears!

Jesus told us –

> "I am the way, the truth and the life!" (Jn 14:6)

> "I have come that they may have life, and have it to the full." (Jn 10:10)

Who could possibly know and say such things—lunatic, or our Lord?

## Free Will and Freedom

We have noted that God created man with a will—a very strong will that enjoys relative freedom. Jesus taught us the true meaning of being free, and He did it, interestingly, at a time when slavery and many forms of servitude were commonplace. To be truly free, we must first be free from the bondage of sin. Jesus understood this, and He offers us the only means of ridding ourselves of our bondage to evil: by replacing it with bondage to what is good, through Him and the Holy Spirit who infuses our heart. As a result, we can only experience true freedom by first restraining our freedom to sin. Then, as we all learn through experience, true freedom can only work if we first acknowledge our obedience to, and our trust in, a loving and holy God.

Accordingly, no concept of freedom arose with Plato, Socrates, or Aristotle, who taught that the State is the highest authority and that the individual must first be subject and obedient to the State. Neither did any concept of freedom come from the Romans, who taught in a fashion similar to the philosophers.

Neither did freedom arise out of the French Revolution, an Orwellian movement leading only to tyranny. Nor did it originate in the AD 600s with Muhammad, whose Qur'an contains not a single reference to individual freedom or free will. Rather, it insists that all become followers or be subject to death.

Likewise, the idea of being free was not born in Great Britain, whose kings during the Middle Ages were the ultimate authority. All laws and even parliament, were subject to the king's edicts. God surely used this situation for good, as it caused the Puritans, Pilgrims, and others to leave Britain and travel to America in an attempt to gain religious freedom. This eventually resulted in the founding of a nation designed to be a new experiment. Men would be governed in what all hoped would be relative freedom, and at the least, they would have religious freedom.

However, neither did freedom originate in 1789 with America's founding nor in 1791 with the first amendment of the US Constitution, which expressly set forth our individual freedoms— including religious freedom or even individual freedom which remains the subject of much controversy to this day.

Perhaps only now, in this postmodern age and latter stage of the "American experience," do we begin to understand that for all to enjoy true freedom in the sense intended by God, we must first limit our freedom by pledging ultimate obedience to a loving and holy God. The alternative is obedience to the rule of self, man, majority rule, or representative government—all made up of men. Do we need any more evidence that placing our trust and obedience in unloving and unholy hands will only limit our freedoms and create unfairness, ill treatment, prejudice, inequality, abuse, and all forms of evil, which only ultimate rule by a loving and holy God can eliminate?[6]

God's love for freedom and for His people to be free and live in peace could not be better illustrated than by all of the amazing steps He took to free Israel from bondage in Egypt. As suggested elsewhere in this book, yet to be experienced in the coming years will be the extent to which God will go in His desire for Israel's protection and peace in the world of today.

The following Scriptures refer to the origination of the concept of freedom:

"In my anguish I cried to the Lord; he answered by setting me *free*" (Ps. 118:5, emphasis added).

---

[6] Samuel, a prophet of God, told us in 1 Samuel 8 about the consequences that man will be subject to when he chooses to be ruled by men (or a king) rather than by God, and how man's rule can only result in greatly restricting the freedoms of all. Both the few and many will greatly limit and burden the freedoms of others. These lessons are more manifest today than ever before, both in America and the world at large.

"I will walk about in *freedom*, for I have sought out your precepts" (Ps. 119:45, emphasis added).

"The spirit of the Sovereign Lord is on me, because the Lord has anointed me to preach the good news to the poor … to proclaim *freedom* for the captives" (Isa. 61:1, emphasis added).

"Now the Lord is the Spirit, and where the Spirit of the Lord is, there is *freedom*" (2 Cor. 3:17, emphasis added).

"If you hold to my teaching … then you will know the truth, and the truth will set you *free*" (John 8:31–32, emphasis added).

"So if the Son sets you *free*, you will be *free* indeed" (John 8:36, emphasis added).

"It is for *freedom* that Christ has set us free … [from] a yoke of slavery" (Gal. 5:1).

"The perfect law that gives *freedom* …" (James 1:25, emphasis added).

## Elimination of Prejudice and Inequality

Just as Jesus came to bring "sight to the blind", so too he came to blind all of us to prejudice and inequality based on race, nationality, gender or status.

Children of God and Sons of Christ are clothed with Christ. "There is neither Jew nor Greek, slave nor free, male nor female, for you are all one in Christ Jesus." [Gal. 3:28]. Children of God are incapable of prejudice or inequality; each and all are seen as one.

Jesus has also taught us to love one another, and in fact, "in humility consider [all] others better than yourselves." [Phil. 2:3]

Many in the world today have logically concluded that to practice prejudice and inequality is impractical, not political, or not conducive to their own well-being, and have therefore "willed" themselves to at least act in a fashion that is seen as without prejudice or inequality. While such conduct is a step in the right direction, it does not come from the heart, and it is not motivated by God's love.

Prejudice and inequality are but two more sins within the evil heart, and without heart regeneration and the Holy Spirit's guidance, the potential for prejudice and unequal treatment will always be present. Teaching and preaching helps but in themselves will never solve the problem or rid people of the sin of prejudice and inequality

Once again, the way to eliminate prejudice and inequality is clear, and perfect, and there is only one way. It is the way taught 1,985 years ago by a 33 year old Jewish man when he said:

"I am the way, the truth and the life."

## Christian Exclusivity?

Like many teens, I imagined myself to be totally incapable of prejudice, injustice, inequality, unfairness, etc., and I was impressed by those who charged Christianity as being "exclusive" and maybe a bit "snobbish" in taking the position that Jesus was the *only* way to the Father and eternal salvation. The argument proceeded to say "it's unfair" and "what about other religions" and "what about those in the world who have never hear the gospel message" and so on.[7]

After opening my heart to the Lord following the suicide death of my earthly Father and as a result of seeking God's wisdom[8] —not mine nor man's—I would offer the following responses to all of these exclusivity claims.

1.  A true God must be both Loving and Holy and such a God would certainly choose to reveal himself to the world, doing so at a propitious time in world history.

---

[7] Actually, the Gospel message is often seen, not heard!

[8] We can all have intelligence, but true wisdom comes only from God. "If any of you lacks wisdom, he should ask God who gives generously to all without finding fault, and it will be given to him" (James 1:5).

For the message of the cross is foolishness to those who are perishing, but to us who are being saved it is the power of God. For it is written...

"I will destroy the wisdom of the wise, the intelligence of the intelligent I will frustrate" (1 Cor. 1:18,19).

Accordingly, note that it is not our "worldly wisdom" that will lead us to the Christ, but God's wisdom and God's leading through the Holy spirit only—so that no one can boast, except in the Lord. (See 1 Cor. 1.)

How better to meaningfully reveal oneself than to be incarnated, and living among the people for 33 years? [9]

How better to prove one's Holiness than by a virgin birth, and dying for the sins of the world?

How better to prove identity than by Resurrection after death, followed by Jesus's Ascension and the coming of the indwelling Holy Spirit?

A propitious time would not be at the beginning nor end of mankind, nor at any time when the events would be unknowable, ignored or lost.

Thus, the chosen time was roughly in the middle of mankind's history, in the geographical middle of the world and world civilization at the time, and a time of relative peace "Pax Romana" and means of travel over Roman built roads.

Did not all of the above incredible and special historical events occur? Are/Were they not each truly unique and from one source?

In addition to all of the above would not a Holy, Just and Loving God reveal Himself and His guidance to us

---

[9] Dream = **D**eity **R**eaching **E**arthlings **A**bout **M**ission

through direct and express communications advising us how to live and act?

Thus –

- God's infallible "word" to us - the <u>Bible:</u> <u>B</u>asic <u>I</u>nstruction <u>B</u>efore <u>L</u>eaving <u>E</u>arth!

- <u>Prayer</u>: Direct line of communication between God and His Children;

- <u>Angels</u>: (remember the important unseen in God's creation) who carry communications and help to us from God; recall Gabriel's appearances to Mary, Joseph, et al;

- <u>Dreams</u>: Recall just a few of God's numerous occasions of communicating through dreams to or through: Joseph, Abraham, Jonah, Daniel, and on and on. [Of course, most dreams, like most TV channels are totally uninfluenced by God!]

Finally, to those who object to a Holy and Just God [instead desiring only a God of "Love", ignoring how wicked man can choose to be] does not God trump all by His greatest act of love, i.e., by forgiving anyone for everything in sole return for our accepting the Son of God's death in our rightful place? As such we surely do have a "Loving All" God!

2.  If there is only *one true God*, it seems logical that there should be only one true *way* to God, and only as He determines. [10]

3.  There is and has been only *one* Son of God, the Christ, who was incarnated and came to earth to teach us and show us *the* way to the Father.

4.  *The* way is singular, *exclusive* of no one—rather it is all inclusive, being open to all—to each and every one of us. It is totally fair, requires no unattainable requirement or circumstance, and is not based on any condition of birth, nationality, station of life, stature, economic status, or deeds performed. In fact, children of God are totally blind to these things.

5.  *The* way is *not forced* on us, and it is not based on unreasoned or irrational decision-making, blind faith, or emotions. Rather, it requires the exercise of our individual and free wills and requires application of our cognitive function to process, assess, and evaluate facts and events—and to be *open* to the leading of the Holy Spirit.

6.  God tells us, "My ways are not your ways." Who are we—the creatures—to question the way(s) of the Creator? In fact, we must forget "our" ways!

---

[10] Truth = **T**he **Reality** **U**ncovered **T**hrough **H**im

7.  Remember that Christianity is not just another "religion." It is a unique relationship with a singularly unique person, the only Son of the one and only God. By its very nature, this relationship must be unique and singular, but otherwise it is "all inclusive."

8.  Finally, while our acceptance of the substitutionary life sacrifice of Jesus is the primary way for us to secure salvation and be assured that one has received salvation, take note that our loving God:

    *   has also promised salvation for those who never heard the gospel message but who placed their faith in God under the Abrahamic covenant, and
    *   finally, has also promised to have "mercy upon whom I will have mercy and ... compassion on whom I will have compassion" (Ex. 33:19). Scripture references those who have come to know God through His created order, nature, conscience, etc., in Romans 1 and 2.

Each spring brings renewal and new life. Seeds that were buried begin to rise and grow into new life. God surely intends this to be nature's sermon on resurrection, renewal, and regeneration. I have often thought that one of God's greatest double meanings is in the daily rising of the sun, which remind us that as the sun rises, so did His Son rise.

## Answering the Question of Christ's Resurrection

While each of us needs to study and answer for ourselves the question of whether Jesus was in fact resurrected, at minimum we should carefully consider three significant points:

1. Several highly experienced lawyers and law professors have considered this subject and have agreed. I am convinced that those who have not yet considered the evidence would also agree. I believe that any jury panel of twelve open-minded laymen considering all the facts and evidence, including any and all contrary arguments, would conclude that Jesus was in fact resurrected. Further, I believe—given all the evidence set forth and referenced in this small summary—that this would be so whether the burden of proof was based on a preponderance of evidence, reasonable probability, or a clear and convincing standard beyond any reasonable doubt (as required in a criminal case). This evidence incorporates all of the traditional and valid evidence accepted in courts of law, including:

   - Multiple eyewitness testimony
   - Ancient creeds or documents
   - Official records
   - Business records
   - Statements or evidence based on dying declarations, present memory, past recollections recorded, exclamatory statements, and *res gestae*.

Further, unlike most legal cases and controversies, virtually all of the relevant and material evidence that exists reflects total unity, consistency, integrity, reality, and quality. It is free of bias[11] and lacks any significant contradictions or reasonable alternative conclusions.[12]

2.  In considering all of the evidence, should one elect *not* to believe that Jesus was resurrected, note well and solemnly that such nonbelief does not, and cannot, change the *fact* that Jesus was resurrected. In our nonbelief, we act at our own peril and cannot escape the all-encompassing and eternal consequences of that nonbelief.

3.  Alternatively, if we conclude that the resurrection of Jesus *is* a fact, then we need to further understand and accept the following consequences of Jesus Christ's resurrection—and what it means to us and to our soul, both here on earth and for eternity:

---

[11] Note that none of the apostles, disciples, or New Testament writers had any financial interest in Christianity or the gospel message. Further, any personal interest would have revolved around saving one's own neck, not sacrificing it!

[12] Some few may still argue that Jesus did not die. They may believe that He was later *resuscitated*. They may believe that Jesus was not resurrected and did not reappear in bodily form, arguing that all of the witnesses were only experiencing illusions or were suffering from hallucinations. I say to them, show me credible evidence—or *any* evidence. The Qur'an suggests two possible explanations in lieu of acknowledging Jesus's death: (1) a substitution (perhaps Judas) in place of Jesus on the cross or (2) some miraculous escape or rescue allowed Jesus by Allah—followed by Jesus's ascension to heaven.

- Jesus is alive today and forever.
- Jesus is the Messiah. He is Jesus the Christ.
- Jesus is the Son of God, and He is God—a triune God in three parts: God the Father, God the Son, and God the Holy Spirit.
- There is only one God, the triune God.
- Jesus Christ is the truth and the only way to the Father, to forgiveness of sin, to salvation of the soul, to a resurrected body, and to life eternal.
- Jesus is unique but not exclusive. He is open to all. He uses not force but rather facts, evidence, the working of the Holy Spirit, and the gift of faith to persuade our very strong and free wills to open our hearts to accepting Him.
- If and when we redirect our will and open our heart to accept Jesus, the Holy Spirit enters in, our human heart is "regenerated," and we become "reborn."[13]
- This heart regeneration can only occur through the indwelling Holy Spirit, which is a gift of God.[14]
- With rebirth, the Spirit within us creates and causes (it can do nothing else!) an overwhelming love for Jesus; a compelling desire to know, obey, and serve Him; and a

---

[13] See Nicodemus's meeting with and question to Jesus: "How can I possibly be born again?" (See John 3:1–19.)

[14] God is spirit and the source of all spirit. While the following is oversimplification for sure, metaphorically picture God's spirit as gasoline, the human heart as a gas tank inside the human body (car), and the human body as the car that requires spirit (gas) in order to run properly and permanently. In order to get this spirit (gas), the human (car) needs the long hose of the Holy Spirit to be inserted into the human heart (tank), thereby infusing the spirit (gas) into the heart (tank). Once infused with the spirit of God, the heart can be redirected toward God and His work.

desire to model one's life after Him in both word and action, with the result that one's life cannot help but bear fruit, like a branch in a grapevine bears grapes.[15]

- With rebirth, we become children of God where there is "neither Jew nor Greek ... slave nor free ... male nor female", where we consider others better than ourselves, and where practice of prejudice or inequality is not possible.

- In rebirth, each new disciple receives the Great Commission and helps effectuate God's kingdom and will here on earth. We recognize that we will fall well short of the perfection that can only be realized under God's reign when heaven finally arrives here on a new earth.

- Finally, with Jesus as the first resurrection, you, your children, and your grandchildren—together with all others who are in Christ and are elected to come to Christ before life's end—will be part of the "second" resurrection. Accordingly, it is by this means, and this means only, that we, our children, and our grandchildren can secure peace, true freedom and equality, total protection, permanent salvation, a resurrected (and perfect) body for all of eternity, and assurance of knowing our destiny!

---

[15] Take caution: mere "acceptance" of Jesus with our lips is insufficient. As R. C. Sproul puts it so well: "We cannot confess what we don't first possess." We must avoid being the barren branch in the grapevine, which the great gardener will prune and is destined for the fire!

## Where Are You Going?

Let none of us be like the great Albert Einstein when he was on a train going to a station somewhere in New York. When the conductor came by and asked for his ticket, he could not find it. Einstein panicked and got down on his hands and knees, desperately searching. The conductor, recognizing the great Einstein, said, "Don't worry. I know who you are, Mr. Einstein, and I'm certain you bought a ticket, so there is no need to search further." Continuing to search desperately, Einstein replied, "Yes, I too know who I am, but I must find my ticket, because I don't know where I am going!"

May God inspire and bless your quest for protection, salvation, peace, equality, freedom, the true meaning of life, and eternity!

# About the Author

The Lord is the "Author" of all that is accurate and true, the rest is the author's.

Wilbur McCoy "Joe" Otto is a graduate of Dickinson College (BA with honors) and the University of Michigan Law School (JD). He was commissioned an officer in the US Regular Army, Judge Advocate Generals Corps, appointed as assistant professor of law at the US Military Academy at West Point, New York.

While at the Academy, Captain Otto was asked to revise the Academy's regulations, and having recently had two daughters born at West Point, he recommended opening the Academy to women candidates, which was approved and implemented by the Department of Army in 1976.

Mr. Otto was assistant professor of economics at Point Park University and assistant professor of health law at the University of Pittsburgh's School of Health and Rehabilitation Sciences for many years. He has served as a faculty member at Trial Advocacy Institutes at the Law Schools of the University of Michigan, University of Pittsburgh, and Duquesne University and for the Pennsylvania Trial Lawyers Association and PA Bar Institute. He is recognized as the first trial lawyer in the United States to utilize video testimony in both state and federal court rooms in 1969 and 1970.

A trial lawyer for fifty years, Mr. Otto is a former CEO of the largest trial/litigation firm in Pittsburgh, Pennsylvania, and presently is with Otto Law Group, LLC. He is a past president of the Academy of Trial Lawyers of Allegheny County, and is a Fellow of the International Society of Barristers and the American Bar Foundation. Mr. Otto is a member of the Bars of Pennsylvania, District of Columbia and the U.S. Supreme Court.

Finally, and most importantly, Mr. Otto, a long-time student of the Bible and biblical history, is the husband of Nancy Ann Fox for fifty-seven years, the father of four children (all lawyers), father-in-law to three more lawyers and grandfather of nine grandchildren. The eldest grandchild, Joshua, is a graduate of the US Naval Academy at Annapolis, and is carrying on the family's unbroken record of military service: the Revolutionary War (John's son, John), the Civil War (Will's father, William, who died at Chickamauga, Tennessee), WWI (Will's son, McDonald, who gave his life), WWII (Charles Fox), the Korean War (brother Richard, wounded), Vietnam War (Joe), and the Lebanon/ Middle East crisis (son, Mark).

# Index

CPSIA information can be obtained at www.ICGtesting.com
Printed in the USA
BVOW05s0439140815

413302BV00001B/2/P

9 781490 883779